Education behind bars

international comparisons

Education behind bars

international comparisons

Edited by Professor William Forster OBE

NIACE

THE NATIONAL ORGANISATION
FOR ADULT LEARNING

This book is dedicated to all those in prison – by choice or not – who are trying to make things better.

Published by the National Institute of Adult Continuing Education
(England and Wales)
21 De Montfort Street, Leicester, LE1 7GE
Company registration no. 2603322
Charity registration no. 1002775

First published 1998
© NIACE

CATALOGUING IN PUBLICATION DATA
A CIP record for this title is available from the British Library
ISBN 1 86201 020 X

Typeset by The Midlands Book Typesetting Company, Loughborough
Cover design by Boldface
Printed in Great Britain by print in black

Contents

Foreword

Prison education has attracted very little attention as a subject in itself. So it is of considerable value to have a book which pulls together prison educators, writing in quite different contexts, with varied national settings.

Prisons, wherever they are, have much in common, and this emerges from almost all the articles in the book. I think it is most clearly set out in that remarkable volume, Vaclav Havel's *Letters to Olga*.

'I used to think prison life must be endless boredom and monotony with nothing much to worry about except the basic problem of making the time pass quickly. But now I've discovered it's not like that. You have plenty of worries here all the time, and though they may seem trivial to the normal world, they are not at all trivial in the prison context. In fact you are always having to chase after something, keep an eye on something, fear for something, hold your ground against something. It's a constant strain on the nerves (someone is always twanging on them), exacerbated by the fact that in many important aspects you cannot behave authentically and must keep your real thoughts to yourself.'

To educate someone in such an atmosphere, or receive useful education, moral, social or academic, involves a remarkable and specialised feat. From China to Peru the background prison culture must be kept in mind, as we read the engrossing story of how it happened.

Sir Stephen Tumim
Previously HM Chief Inspector of Prisons

Introduction

When invitations to contribute to this volume were issued, quite deliberately, few guidelines were stipulated apart from asking that contributors should give some indication of the philosophy within which their national prison education system had been formulated and that some reference should be made to how this worked out in practice. The consequence has been a refreshingly wide variety of approaches which should serve to stimulate further contacts in, and work on, more focused areas. Two major influences motivated the editor. The first was his experience over many years of visiting conferences and seminars in many countries, hearing of many exciting and worthwhile endeavours, and yet being aware that the bundle of papers he brought home were rarely distributed beyond immediate participants. It seemed valuable to make a modest contribution to what should be a much more developed international discussion.

The second was the editor's awareness of the relative isolation of many of those working within the prison walls, many of whom are not fortunate enough to be able to meet colleagues from other countries. Prisons are, by definition, closed and the sense of confinement can affect staff as much as inmates. Moreover, when public opinion swings against rehabilitative activity for the convicted, and when resources are tight, the sense of isolation is reinforced by the sense that one is undervalued. But not only is the work of educators in prisons at risk of being at best ignored, at worst disparaged, by the public at large; its closed institutional nature has often resulted in separation from the mainstream of adult education. The truth is that many of the new initiatives we have all seen highlighted in recent years – the development of basic skills, the urgency of vocational education and its wedding to an element of social education, special programmes for the educationally disadvantaged, for example – all these have been the bread and butter of prison educators for many years. It's not just a case of offering more professional support to prison educators from the mainstream – it's a case of realising that this sector of activity has a wealth of expertise to offer were more of us aware that it existed. So the purpose of this collection is to raise awareness rather than to offer a definitive statement: and the variety of approaches and attitudes herein is designed to catch a variety of interested eyes rather than to allow strict comparisons to be made.

The variety arises partly from the different standpoints of the various authors. Some are academics, usually employed with a wider remit in higher education; they are in a position to take a thoughtful overview and combine this with a polemic stance. A strong case for the cause needs to be made and examples of this will be found in these pages. Others are involved more directly in the prison education service, usually at a policy-forming or administrative level; here we find contrasting attitudes. There are those who are working in well developed systems, who see a hardening of public attitudes and consequent withdrawal of sympathy on the part of politicians as well as a diminution of resources — and they are pessimistic. There are those who are fighting, not so much for the survival of the system as for its successful birth; whilst they have often no resources at all and an uphill political battle to fight, a refreshing optimism peeps through between the lines.

But the greatest variety, of course, emerges from the historical and cultural setting within which each writer is working; most papers find it necessary to establish what it is that has brought about what is happening now before the present situation can be described. The North American and Australian papers emerge from a context where clear, albeit different and sometimes hostile, polices have been formed at national level and the authors are in position to extrapolate from this a set of concepts against which practice can be measured; England and Wales has a similar history of stop-go, but with a much less clear concept of 'corrections' or sense of direction — it is only to be hoped that recent reorganisation and increased systematisation does not stifle the traditional blend of professionalism and individual initiative which has achieved so much in the past. The paper from China underlines the dependency of the activity on traditional, cultural perceptions; at first glance, the dominance of language may appear alien to the rest of us but this, I suggest, is to deceive ourselves. A survey of any set of newspaper headlines demonstrates how our attitudes to any major public issue — particularly crime and its treatment — are dominated by the power of the word.

Most of the papers are concerned with a hardening of public attitudes towards deviance and the treatment of deviants, and the way in which politicians have had to respond to this. The rehabilitative services in prisons would seem to have taken more than their fair share of the international pulling back from the expenditure of public money, and it is difficult to imagine private purses being opened for this purpose — there's not a great deal of publicity or glamour to be found within those walls. The paper from the Netherlands, long lauded as having an enlightened system, underlines this plight with vigour. If resources available to prison services diminish, and the public make the demand that more and higher walls are to be built, then the effect on positive activity within those walls is damaging.

The papers from Eastern Europe are particularly interesting, demonstrating widely different stances and problems within a rapidly changing political context. Latvia — whilst modest about its situation — reveals heroic attempts to fill a vacuum, both of provision and legislative, left by a retreating regime, whilst beset by severe economic problems; Poland shows an integration with the public education system which must be the envy of many; Germany, with a developed tradition, not only had to repair the gaps left by the events of the 1930s and 1940s, but also has now to face the Herculean task of re-uniting East and West and coping with the consequent effects on the penal system as a whole and treatment within. What does emerge from each of these papers is a warming sense of personal enthusiasm, whether that enthusiasm springs from a sense of social duty, a personal sense of outrage, a professional sense that students should be looked after, or a liberal instinct for human rights.

There is also the sense — although it is not articulated in every case — that societies in general have not got it right; that education and training is a necessary antidote to imprisonment, for, in general, this latter process makes things worse, not better, both for society and for the individual. Education should not need to be an antidote to prison, it should be a complement and on of the dangers of a book such as this is that it treats of education as a separate activity within prison (which, unfortunately, it often is) instead of an integrated part of penal practice. It is only when the public and politicians together work out what prison is for, and realise that the mutual concepts of human warehouses and constant recidivism are not just inhumane but are, in the long term, economically foolhardy that those whose work is represented by the papers in this collection will be able to command the support and the praise they deserve. For, isolated at times as they may be, they are working on behalf of all of us.

Bill Forster
University of Leicester, 1998

Chapter One

Policy development and cultural issues in Australian prison education

Bob Semmens, Department of Education Policy and Management, University of Melbourne, Australia

This chapter will detail the current situation in relation to provision of education for prisoners in Australia. The major focus of the discussion will be on recent developments in the State of Victoria whose system for education and training of prisoners is best known to the author. Reference to other States will be made for comparison or for innovative developments which are not part of, or not emphasised as much, in the Victorian system. Reference will also be made to developments in education provision for young offenders and offenders on community-based orders where such developments are new and of interest to an international audience.

Distance has always been a problem for programme delivery and co-ordination in every State and Territory, although not to such an extent in Victoria and Tasmania which are smaller States. While educational programmes of some kind are available in all prisons in Australia, the vast size of the country, combined with the concentration of population in the south east of the continent, means that the range of programmes available is broader in the larger prisons in the capital cities and the more densely populated areas to the south and east. Prisoner numbers in prisons in other countries may make it more economical to deliver a wide range of programmes in these countries. By contrast, it is unusual for any prison in Australia to accommodate more than 1,000 prisoners and some prisons in the far north and west of Australia accommodate considerably fewer than 100 prisoners. Even so, quite comprehensive education and training programmes are provided in some prisons with small numbers of prisoners.

Each State and Territory has its own corrections' administration, each with its own system for delivery of education and training programmes. Generally, though, it can be said that the major emphasis is on basic literacy and numeracy, with an increasing sophistication in vocational training. There is also increasing refinement of programmes for prisoners with non-English-speaking backgrounds, but provision for Aboriginal prisoners is still largely inadequate, because there are few Aboriginal teachers and there is an issue of the cultural relevance of many programmes that are offered.

This is a serious problem for correctional administrators and educators because Aboriginal people are imprisoned at around 17 times the rate of non-Aboriginal people, ranging from 24:1 in Western Australia to 4:1 in Tasmania (Australian Bureau of Statistics, 1996). It is probably the most persistently serious problem that the various governments in Australia have never faced with much resolve or dedication.

Other problems with education and training provision are less serious, but since 1994 they are harder to identify, because the Australian Institute of Criminology ceased to publish comparative data on ethnic background, levels of schooling, previous employment/unemployment details and recidivism rates. The same applies to young offenders and to offenders on community-based orders. It is therefore not a simple matter to apply a recidivism criterion to programme outcomes. As there is no Commonwealth co-ordinating role, offender profile data must now be sought separately from each State correctional authority. Differences in definition of terms and categories of prisoner complicate some comparisons. However, in the area of prison education, information is readily available from recent reports, conferences and other published material and will now be available from the Australian Bureau of Statistics.

Despite these problems and limitations, there have been many improvements in the quality and range of education and training programmes in prisons in recent years. These developments will be discussed in the following pages, beginning with a brief overview of general developments in education and training in Australia, which have influenced the direction of correctional programmes, then going on to look more closely at the situation in Victoria and innovative programmes in other parts of Australia.

Recent Australian education policy developments

Traditionally, schools in Australia have provided a broad general education during the compulsory years, with some increasing specialisation in the post-compulsory years as preparation for those students who wish to proceed to a post-secondary qualification at a technical college or university. The numbers of young people seeking tertiary education have increased dramatically in recent years and about 25 per cent of qualified applicants are unable to gain places in the tertiary sector (*Age* newspaper, 29 May 1996). The increased demand for tertiary education is partly due to high youth unemployment rates, re-structuring of the workforce and greater job opportunities for tertiary graduates.

The higher school retention rates are also due to the increasing emphasis of education policy on post-compulsory education. This trend is clearly observable from 1987, when the then Commonwealth Minister for Employment, Education and Training (John Dawkins) responded to the Kirby *Inquiry Into Labour Market Programs* (1985) with his statement in which he addressed the issue of how education and training would play a more active role in the process of economic adjustment. While school retention rates had risen from 36.3 per cent in 1982 to 48.7 per cent in 1986, they were to rise to 65 per cent in the early 1990s. In fact, in Victoria the retention rate rose to 85 per cent in 1993 (*Age* newspaper, 14 October 1995), creating a huge problem for a system which, while it had diversified its curriculum in the post-compulsory years, was now straining to make the links between schooling and further education, training, or employment.

The Commonwealth had foreseen this problem to some extent following the Dawkins statement and commissioned several reports (Finn, 1991; Carmichael, 1992; Mayer, 1992; Deveson, 1992) which attempted to show how 'pathways' to employment could be created through closer co-ordination between Colleges of Technical and Further Education (TAFE), schools and workplaces. Students are now able to gain 'dual recognition' for some courses taken in the post-compulsory years – that is, recognition of subjects within the final year of school certificate for credit towards a TAFE qualification, as well as qualifying for university entrance. This arrangement may also include related work experience. The Mayer (1992) key competencies for participation in the workforce, combined with the Carmichael levels of skill for advancement in the workforce, provided a structure for the 'pathways' concept. The structure also provides for flexibility in 'pathways' and a diversity of destinations. For many students, however, leaving school is still like moving into uncharted waters (Dwyer, 1995). The best known and most popular pathways amongst young people are the traditional routes to university or apprenticeship. What is clear though, from the tremendous amount of activity in connecting school and work, is that the post-compulsory schooling system is more closely vocational than in the past, that competition for available jobs is more fierce and that continual updating of qualifications will be necessary in a world which no longer promises secure lifetime employment for the great majority of workers.

To assist the States in their adjustments to, and co-ordination of, education and training arrangements, the Commonwealth established the Australian National Training Authority (ANTA) in 1992, following an agreement by Commonwealth, State and Territory Heads of Government to develop a national system of vocational education and training (VET). This national system comprises all those who are providing or using vocational education and training in both the private and public sectors. The Commonwealth provides substantial funding towards meeting nationally-agreed training priorities and achieving consistency and portability in training qualifications between both States and training providers. Each State and Territory has a training authority responsible for planning local training efforts within the overall national VET sector. These authorities ensure that local training courses are consistent with national strategies, that course accreditation is according to national standards, and that a State or Territory training profile is developed in consultation with local industries, their employees and other relevant parties.

Further, in 1995, the Commonwealth established, under ANTA, the Australian Vocational Training System (AVTS), which is a system of competency-based, entry-level training which can be delivered by secondary schools, TAFE Colleges, private providers and industry. The AVTS covers all aspects of vocational education and training and leads to the development of skills at the point of entry to, or the initial stages of, employment.

Particular groups of people whose needs have not always been identified or incorporated into vocational education and training programme provision are now targeted by ANTA. These targeted groups are: women; Aboriginal and Torres Strait Islanders; people without adequate social, literacy and numeracy skills; people with disabilities; rural people; unemployed people; and people from a non-English-speaking background. While prisoners are not specifically mentioned, they are strongly represented amongst most of the targeted groups for special programme provision.

Indeed, the overall education policy direction in Australia has been reflected in developments in prison education. As the next section will show, the field of correctional education has certainly not been left out of the Australia-wide trend towards emphasising vocational training and its co-ordination over the last decade.

Impact of national education policy changes upon prison education programmes

Over the past decade there has been considerable interest in education in prisons from a variety of sources. The impetus for change and improvement was first noticeable in Victoria when the *Ministerial Review of Educational Services to the Disabled* (1984) contained a recommendation that TAFE Colleges 'assume full responsibility for education centres in prisons' (Rec 4.7.2). Action on this recommendation was to see prisoner education taken out of the schools division special education section in 1989 and placed into the vocationally-oriented community colleges for post-school-age students, called TAFE.

The Victorian TAFE recommendation came in the context of government policies at State and Commonwealth level for increased access to education and training for disadvantaged groups. Following Dawkins' *Skills For Australia* (1987), which placed strong emphasis on access to vocational training for economic adjustment, various programmes were established to facilitate training and re-training for labour market opportunities, including considerations of possible implications for prison education. In 1988 the State Training Board commissioned the author to undertake a study of vocational training in Victorian prisons (Semmens, 1988). The report detailed how links could be established between prison education centres, prison industries, and local TAFE colleges so that prisoners could combine on-the-job and off-the-job credit towards community-recognised vocational qualifications. At the same time, a consultative committee was established, consisting of representatives of the State Training Board, the Office of Corrections, and the Technical Teachers Union to work out co-ordination arrangements.

The outcome was the establishment of Corrections as an industry within the State Training Board. This facilitated training funds through TAFE colleges to prisons, in the same way as funds would be provided to colleges for training in any other industry such as building construction or hospitality. Associated with this development was the re-constitution of prison education centres as campuses of an identified TAFE College. The Corrections Industry Training Board was officially constituted within the State Training Board in 1991 and since then it has produced an annual Corrections Industry Training Plan which sets out goals, programme priorities and resource requirements for the next year as well as reporting on its achievements in the preceding year.

At the same time there was increased interest in correctional education in other States as well, most notably in Queensland where the Byrne Report (1991) strongly criticised the range and quality of education programmes in Queensland prisons. While the criticism of inadequate resources and access was general, special mention was made of the need for establishment of task forces to develop appropriate programmes for Aboriginal prisoners, women and juveniles. There have been substantial improvements in education and work programmes in Queensland prisons since 1991. These improvements have been part of an overall upgrading of outdated facilities in that State, and additional impetus has been derived from a number of other reports and conferences on the subject of education and training in correction institutes.

In 1991, the (Commonwealth) Senate Standing Committee on Employment, Education and Training conducted an Inquiry into Adult and Community Education. Its report, *Come In Cinderella*, observed that:

> *of all the disadvantaged people who face barriers to their participation in further education and training, those in the prison system are among the most neglected (p 113).*

The Report supported Byrne's recommendation that all prisoners, not just those in Queensland, be eligible for fee relief and a book allowance from the Commonwealth Government. This recommendation has yet to be acted on, despite a similar recommendation being repeated at every national conference and report on correctional education since 1991.

Two separate conferences took place in early 1992, one in Perth under the auspices of the Australian Institute of Criminology in association with the Civil Rehabilitation Council of Western Australia (Outcare), the other in Brisbane, organised by a former prisoner and sponsored by Qantas and the Queensland Corrections Commission. Such interest had never been shown in correctional education in Australia before. The Perth conference attracted 150 participants from across Australia and made recommendations directed at developing national standards and funding from the Commonwealth Government. There was strong Aboriginal participation and the conference urged the Commonwealth Government to implement the findings of the Royal Commission into Aboriginal Deaths in Custody (1991). At the same time the conference protested that while the conference was in session, the Western Australian Government passed legislation enabling courts to imprison joyriders, most of whom were teenage Aboriginal youths.

The Queensland conference also heard of the particular problems of Aboriginals in custody but as it had focussed on international participants from New Zealand, the United States and Canada, there was resistance to passing any resolutions urging improvement in programmes for Aboriginal prisoners. Instead, the conference heard of the cognitive skills programmes being developed in Canada and went on an excursion to the newly-opened Borallon prison, Australia's first private prison. This was not altogether a diversion from dealing with important current Australian issues in prison education as the visitors saw, amongst other interesting programmes, a very exciting Aboriginal education programme under the leadership of an outstanding Aboriginal teacher.

The conference also expressed strong support for the recently-established Melbourne University branch of the International Forum on Education in Penal Systems (IFEPS). It also expressed support for the Perth conference recommendation that the Commonwealth establish a national clearinghouse for research, policy and programme data on correctional education.

Both of these conferences in Perth and Brisbane provided opportunities for the author to interview participants for his commissioned project on correctional education and training on behalf of the National Board on Employment Education and Training (NBEET). This project investigated employment and training opportunities for prisoners and ex-prisoners. In addition to the interviews in Perth and Brisbane, day-long seminars were conducted in Melbourne, Adelaide and Sydney. The report (*NBEET Commissioned Report No 17, 1992*) recommended that the Commonwealth recognise prison time as unemployment time in terms of meeting criteria for inclusion in labour market programmes after release. This would mean that ex-prisoners would not have to wait six to twelve months for admission to job training programmes for long-term unemployed people. It was argued that most prisoners were long-term unemployed before going to prison and were likely to be long-term unemployed after release, if they did not have immediate access to employment programmes upon release. It was also recommended that States run properly-accredited programmes in correctional facilities to increase the chances of prisoners gaining employment upon release, thus reducing the numbers of ex-prisoners needing to move into Commonwealth labour market programmes.

Later in 1992, the Commonwealth Department of Employment, Education and Training (DEET) commissioned the Australian Institute of Criminology to undertake a national study of pre-release and post-release schemes to ascertain the best features of such programmes. The project was funded from the Aboriginal Deaths in Custody budget to implement the findings of the Royal Commission. The report, *Keeping Them In, Keeping Them Out* (1992), stressed the need:

> to improve co-ordination of education and training opportunities across Australia, and to enable pathways which provide continuity between the prison system and the outside world to operate. Until these changes are made, the desired impact of education and training on recidivism rates is unlikely to be realised (p 71).

The report also recommended that high priority be given to improving prisoner access to education and training, continuity of participation between prisons and from prison to community, improved communication between custodial and education staff and recognition of the value of peer tutelage, especially for Aboriginal prisoners. While the report indicated support for the NBEET study's recommendation that the Commonwealth increase prisoner access to Commonwealth labour market programmes, no specific recommendation was made in this regard.

However, DEET did call together heads of all state corrections departments, education providers and three former Aboriginal prisoners, to prepare a response to the education and training recommendations of the Royal Commission into Aboriginal Deaths in Custody. This two-day conference took place late in 1993 in Canberra and was attended by the former Royal Commissioner, Mr Hal Wootton. While the *Keeping Them In, Keeping Them Out* report aimed to address Royal Commission Recommendation 110, which related to best practice, the Canberra conference mainly addressed Recommendation 185:

> That the Department of Employment, Education and Training be responsible for the development of a comprehensive national strategy designed to improve the opportunities for the education of those in custody.

The conference made similar recommendations to previous reports emphasising the need for programme access, continuity, accreditation, and labour market relevance of credentials. It also stressed the importance of non-award personal development programmes and drew attention to the need for culturally-appropriate programmes, quoting from the World Indigenous Peoples' Conference at Woollongong (1993), which was held at about the same time as the Canberra conference, and issued the following statement, known as the *Coolangatta Statement* (1993), which referred in part to the importance of self-determination in Indigenous education, including the right to:

control/govern Indigenous education systems; establish schools and other learning facilities that recognise, respect and promote indigenous values, philosophies, and ideologies; develop and implement culturally inclusive curricula; utilise the essential wisdom of indigenous elders in the education process; establish the criterion for educational evaluation and assessment; define and identify standards for the gifted and talented; promote the use of Indigenous languages in education; establish the parameters and ethics within which Indigenous education research should be conducted; design and deliver culturally appropriate and sensitive teacher training; participate in teacher certification and selection; develop criteria for the registration and operation of schools and other learning facilities; and, choose the nature and scope of education without prejudice (Rec 2.2.4).

Unfortunately DEET did not act on the recommendations of the Canberra conference and a year later the Commonwealth House of Representatives Standing Committee on Aboriginal and Torres Strait Islander Affairs was strongly critical of DEETs tardiness, as well as the limited nature of the Australian Institute of Criminology study. It called for a comprehensive national study of the education and training needs of Aboriginal and Torres Strait Islanders in custody, in consultation with Aboriginal and Torres Strait Islanders, not just prison administrators (*Justice Under Scrutiny*, paras 9.39–9.47). The study has not yet been undertaken although some Aboriginal liaison positions were created to support Aboriginal prisoner transition to community. The positions have never been advertised. The recent change of Commonwealth Government, with consequent downsizing of DEET, makes the prospect of filling the positions appear unlikely in the short-term at least.

Meanwhile, there has been some progress in other areas. In March 1994, Melbourne IFEPS held its first national conference. There were participants from other IFEPS centres but the issues for discussion were specifically on Australian developments in employment, education and training of offenders. The conference noted that ANTA, recently established in January 1994, had the task of implementing the National Training Reform Agenda, which included the development of agreed competency standards for industrial work requirements; competency-based training; curriculum development; flexible programme delivery and assessment; and recognition of prior learning. The conference also noted that while the ANTA had a mandate to increase access of disadvantaged groups to training, there was no specific mention of offenders. The conference therefore called for the offender group to be included in the National Training Reform Agenda (*IFEPS Conference Proceedings*, 1994:427). The conference also reiterated previous calls for improved access, co-ordination, continuity, accreditation of culturally appropriate education for offenders and for improved access to labour market programmes upon release. There were also recommendations for the establishment of minimum standards for programme evaluation and yet another call for a national clearinghouse of best national and international practice.

In general, 1995 was a better year. Firstly, the IFEPS recommendations were taken up by the Commonwealth Senate Employment, Education and Training References Committee, which established an Inquiry into Education and Training in Correctional Facilities in January 1995. Submissions were received from around Australia and interviews were conducted in many places, including prisons. Secondly, during the course of the year, DEET extended its labour market programme eligibility to prisoners during the pre-release phase of their sentence. Certain conditions applied but nevertheless this was a substantial breakthrough which acknowledged the recommendations of reports and representations from State governments over recent years.

The second IFEPS national conference at Hobart in November 1995 was pleased to receive a progress report from the Senate committee indicating special concern about prisoner access to programmes, especially literacy and numeracy. The progress report also highlighted the need for improved co-ordination and support for transition to community living in general health and welfare, as well as education and training. As the Senate committee had not finalised its work, the conference decided to forward its major findings to the committee for its consideration (*IFEPS Conference Proceedings*, 1995). Specifically, the conference called for funding for research and publication of models of best practice in correctional education and training and reiterated previous calls for the establishment of a national clearinghouse, possibly in conjunction with other IFEPS centres and an international sponsor.

The final Senate Inquiry report was published in April 1996. While it did not specifically endorse a national clearinghouse, it did recommend that ANTA establish a secretariat to co-ordinate and monitor the implementation of a national strategy for offenders until the year 2000 (Rec 5c), and that ANTA fund the National Centre for Vocational Education Research to develop a database in corrections education (Rec 9b). Additionally, the Senate report recommended that the Australian Institute of Criminology develop a draft set of national standards for education and training of people in custody (Rec 4), and that the National Corrective Services Administrators' Conference establish a schedule of annual conferences of correctional educators (Rec 32b).

The above recommendations characterise the report. In various areas of concern the report proposes solutions through utilising or extending existing agencies and resources, even including contributions from prisoners in defining their education and training needs (Rec 1), and proposing that education and training of offenders be included in the accountability and performance requirements of prison managers (Rec 3). The theme of co-ordinating existing agencies and resources also extends to the post-release period:

> *The Committee recommends that each State and Territory, with support from the relevant Commonwealth agencies (Commonwealth Employment Service, Department of Social Security etc), develop a 'through-care' strategy for offender management which extends into the post-release period, and which is predicated on the co-operation of, and co-ordination between, the corrections, education, welfare and offender-support agencies beyond the prison gate (Rec 26).*

There is still a long way to go before any of the Senate Inquiry recommendations are implemented. While the Committee had representation of the major political parties, there has been a change of Government and the new Government's mandate did not include anything about offender education. Additionally, the States are traditionally very protective of their own powers and will not have Commonwealth priorities imposed on them easily. It is therefore up to the various groups who contributed to the Inquiry to develop priorities and collaborative strategies for convincing governments and agencies to implement key recommendations. So far, the Inquiry has been the means of bringing together changes for the better over the last decade and focussing attention on what is possible over the next few years. The next IFEPS conference in 1997 decided to focus on community transition, highlighting best practice in pre-release and post-release programmes for community reintegration.

Consolidating change in Victoria

Community reintegration is generally an underdeveloped area, even if obvious for maximum programme and individual success. The handing back of full citizenship responsibility at the prison gate is difficult for the system and prisoners to manage, so it has been neglected. Who will take responsibility for what is a much easier proposition while the prisoner is inside because the system is totally responsible. Upon release, the prisoner is often caught between the ecstasy of freedom and the pain of what to do next to act his or her age in a world that has changed in the interim. The sense of being watched takes a long time to fade and this raises anxiety levels of ex-prisoners, particularly those who have no supportive relationships.

This problem is now starting to be addressed in Victoria, because the education and training system is now sufficiently sophisticated and has the infrastructure support necessary for further innovative developments. These last few years have seen the development of excellent vocational training programmes which are modularised, co-ordinated and industry-accredited. It would be a pity to see the quality spoiled by lack of attention to follow-through options and support for prisoners. As preparation for this next stage of programme development, the consortium of senior TAFE managers has undertaken its own evaluation of progress to date, in the implementation of training programme pathways. That is, the extent to which prisoners have been able to pursue a particular course as they move from one prison to another, from one level of security to another, and from prison to community supervision (Wilson and Penaluna, 1995). In this study 115 prisoners were 'tracked' for three months and some problems identified. Feedback to the prison managers has brought remedial action to internal arrangements for prisoner transfers. However, the major concern arising from the 'tracking' exercise was that, of the 39 prisoners in the sample who were released, only three continued their studies beyond release. This finding is consistent with the outcome studies by the author on male and female post-release experience (Semmens, 1991; Semmens, 1996) in which it was found that, despite their best intentions, post-release responsibilities and weak social networks make it very difficult for most prisoners to contemplate further study or training.

This is not to say that community programmes are difficult to access. Rather, it is to say that more pressing immediate survival issues occupy more time and energy than could have been foreseen whilst in prison – issues such as accommodation, employment, personal relationships and family responsibilities, coming to terms with a spoiled reputation and possibly community resistance to normalisation of community membership. The corrections system in Victoria has been working at the problem over recent years. Each regional community corrections office has, since 1992, developed a regional industry plan to reflect the objectives of the annual departmental Corrections Industry Training Plan (Roberts and Wilmott, 1994). These plans identify the education and training needs of offenders in the region; the range and diversity of accredited training, labour market and further education programmes available in the region; and regional priorities in the requirements for accredited training programmes linked to employment opportunities. It is now possible for parolees or offenders on community corrections orders to combine authorised unpaid community work as the practical component for certain accredited courses. Time spent in courses of related study can also be deducted from the time to be served on a community corrections order.

Another scheme, which is gathering some momentum, is the delivery of workplace-based education. This enables groups of offenders to study at the community worksite and reduces anxiety about failure often associated with attending a formal education institution.

Taking the idea of education and training delivery to where the clients are, physically and psychologically, some TAFE Colleges are now extending informal education environments to young unemployed people who did not complete secondary schooling (Fairman and Wilson, 1995). Participation is voluntary and may include unpaid work, paid work experience, education and training, vocational awareness, personal development, and case management. The exact components offered will vary according to youth needs and the resources of the community agency involved. The aim is to prepare alienated young people for re-entry to more formal education and training programmes, as well as develop confidence in themselves and their competence to participate in the workforce.

One such programme is run in an inner city area of Melbourne. Kangan TAFE, in association with the Salvation Army, has established the project called 'Bridging Education and Training' (BEAT). The project has attracted about 20 young people in the 15-to-24 age group, of whom some are homeless, most have been at least on the edge of crime, possibly to support a drug habit and all have had negative school experience. Over a period of about six months, participants can gain a Certificate of General Education for Adults (CGEA) and take a course in planning for employment and training. The essence of the programme is its 'hands on' approach to learning and skill acquisition. The work experience aspect of the programme is within a commercial business that is safe and supportive while providing a training wage. It is claimed (Brooker, 1996) that participants gain self-esteem by taking responsibility for the product of their work and then selling it to the public. Upon completion of this informal programme, participants are either eligible for admission to the Kangan TAFE, or are assisted in making arrangements for return to secondary college. The participants are also familiarised with Commonwealth labour market programme options. The next step, of course, is to match the efforts to increase access to education and training programmes with increased accessibility and co-ordination of health and welfare agencies and resources.

Developments in other states

The CGEA was originally developed in Victoria, but is now used in New South Wales, South Australia and Western Australia as well. It is divided into four streams at four levels – reading and writing, oral communications, numerical concepts, and general curriculum options. In each stream at each level there are modules of study which may vary from 10 to 50 hours. A certificate is awarded upon completion of each stream of study at each level.

The CGEA has given prison education a general education pathway. Using a competency sheet, each student's progress is recorded and transferred with him/her to another prison or to another provider upon release so that she/he can take up where she/he left off without delay. Curriculum moderation is used to formalise and maintain standards through gaining agreement between practitioners about set assessment tasks and the framework competencies. Internal, external and state-wide moderation is compulsory to ensure that all practitioners are interpreting the competency criteria in the same way.

In South Australia, the Department of Correctional Services has a licence to provide the CGEA because the Department, rather than an external authority (such as TAFE in Victoria), is responsible for education and training of prisoners. From its annual education budget, the Department buys programmes from

TAFE and other providers. Since taking over the responsibility for education and training provision in 1994, the Department has supported a range of developments, from pre-vocational programmes in horticulture, engineering and business studies through to a pre-release labour market programme called 'kick-start.' While it is reported (Meatheringham, 1995) that prisoners appreciate the vocational emphasis of programmes, they also want increased access to programmes which address personal development issues, such as anger management, substance abuse, parenting, cognitive skills, life skills and health (Tierney, 1996: 93). There is also an increasing demand for education and training amongst prisoners, which may be an indicator of the quality and perceived relevance of the programmes that are currently offered.

As in South Australia, the co-ordination of prison education in New South Wales is undertaken from within the Department of Corrective Services, but in a different way — by the recently-created Adult Education and Vocational Training Institute (AEVTI). All accredited programmes are delivered to correctional facilities through AEVTI, be it TAFE, DEET, community college or any other selected provider. All vocational awards are made on AEVTI letterheads. AEVTI also takes responsibility for portability of training from one prison to another and for awarding recognition of prior learning.

The other significant and different development in NSW prison education is the number of high quality teaching resource packages specially designed for inmates, including some in the basic literacy course, which have been produced by prisoners on topics of interest to themselves and other prisoners learning to read.

In Queensland the education of prisoners is the responsibility of each correctional facility. The Queensland Corrective Services Commission (QCSC) employs education officers to co-ordinate programmes for prisoners at each centre and each centre has its own budget for determining its own programme profile. Within the QCSC there is a Vocational Education and Training Advisory Body (VETAB) which attracts funds from the Queensland Vocational Education, Training and Employment Commission (VETEC) and articulates the training of offenders within the State Training Profile. However, the most pressing need of prisoners is for basic literacy and numeracy and, to this end, a Certificate of Vocational Access has been established in conjunction with TAFE and is available in distance mode to all prisons in Queensland. Co-ordination of programme participation begins upon admission where a case management plan is prepared for every prisoner with a sentence of at least nine months, or less if special needs are identified. Special programmes have also been developed in anger management, substance abuse and cognitive skills to meet the expressed needs of prisoners.

Another feature of the Queensland prison system is the development of the Western Outreach Camps (WORC) scheme, whereby up to 180 prisoners nearing release can transfer to a work team of about 25 prisoners at one of nine country camps. They participate in local projects in consultation with the local community advisory committees and their respective needs for community amenities.

There is also a strong emphasis on development of good work habits in Tasmania where all prisoners are expected to work during the day and attend classes at night if they wish to continue their education or develop hobby skills. In cases where certain classes can only be conducted during the day, prisoners may participate at no cost to their daily pay rate. Despite the small number of prisoners (about 250 spread over six prisons and mostly with short sentences), a wide range of courses is offered from basic education to vocational training and tertiary courses through distance education. Various funding sources from other Tasmanian government departments and from the Commonwealth government are distributed through the prison corrections programme co-ordinator in consultation with the Prison Education and Training Steering Committee.

The Northern Territory stands out from the rest of Australia partly because it still does not have full statehood, but also because it has the highest Aboriginal population and a very high proportion of Aboriginal prisoners. There are about 450 prisoners in the Northern Territory and around 75 per cent are Aboriginal or Torres Strait Islanders. More than 80 per cent of Aboriginal prisoners speak languages other than English as their first language. This presents a problem for the NT Department of Correctional Services because, while it has taken responsibility for education and vocational training, access to modules and courses through the national TAFE network does not meet the special education and training needs of a large proportion of prisoners. Some funds are available from the Commonwealth for Aboriginal programmes and there is an Aboriginal steering committee which has responsibility for advising and endorsing Aboriginal programme funding allocations.

The issue of providing appropriate and adequate programmes for Aboriginal prisoners is reflected to a varying degree in every prison administration in Australia. Insufficient programmes, insufficient Aboriginal teachers, cultural differences, not only between black and white, but also between various tribal groups, are just some of the problems that need to be addressed in programme design and delivery. As one Aboriginal teacher in a New South Wales prison (Byrne, 1995) has written:

> Aboriginality is about culture, identity, shared experience and world view. It is not about physical traits and stereotypes.
> Consultation avoids exploitation of Aboriginal people.
> Consultation recognises Aboriginal people as the authorities on Aboriginal culture.

Prison administrations, like other government departments, are still struggling to consult and then to provide culturally-appropriate services to Aboriginal people, whether those services are education and training, health, welfare, housing or whatever, and whether those services are in prison or in the wider community. Still Aboriginal people die in custody at the same rate as they did prior to the Royal Commission which reported in 1991.

One wonders also about the trend towards private prisons in Australia. Modularised vocational training programmes may be incorporated into private prisons, but it is less clear how private prisons may improve programme provision for Aboriginal prisoners. In the main, this is because private prisons lack the resources and capacity for collaboration and co-ordination of the state departments and it is unlikely that they will have budgetary flexibility within their single prison administrations to provide special programmes for small groups of prisoners. Further, private prison consortia in Australia have so far been dominated by English or American companies and this could complicate the cultural issues for education and training programmes for Aboriginal prisoners as well as other prisoners.

The Victorian Commissioner for Correctional Services, Mr. John Van Groningen, claims (1995) that the excellent model for education and training developed over recent years in Victoria will be continued and extended to the private prisons currently being built, and will house more than half of the prison population of 2,500 prisoners by the end of 1996. In Victoria the training pathways across prisons and into the community, the state-wide consistency of course provision, the training priorities and the co-ordination and co-operation of a variety of agencies will include private prisons. The Commissioner makes no specific mention of programmes for Aboriginal prisoners, but the Victorian prison system has a much smaller proportion of Aboriginal prisoners than any mainland State and therefore the problem is not so obvious in Victoria. Admittedly, in Queensland, there appears to be some special effort to cater for Aboriginal prisoners in the private Borallon prison. It remains to be seen whether such special effort is maintained and replicated in other private prisons in Queensland and other States. Due to the confidentiality requirement of private prison contracts, the programme provision specifications for Aboriginal prisoners, or any group of prisoners, are unknown. We can only wait and hope that programme evaluation will be possible and influential.

Conclusion

This chapter has reviewed developments in prison education in Australia, especially over the last decade, which has been a very active and largely positive period of reform. The major emphasis on vocational training has reflected the general direction of Australian education policy. In relation to prison education and training, the chapter has identified a large number of innovative developments and two areas are identified for increased attention. These two areas are Aboriginal education and training, and the need for improved transition arrangements from prison to community for all prisoners. While much work has been done from time to time, sustained focus is essential if the 'good old Aussie' principle of 'a fair go for everyone' is to be fully realised in relation to prisoner rehabilitation and community protection.

References

'Age' Newspaper, (14 October 1995). *School Retention Rates in Australia*, Melbourne.

'Age' Newspaper, (29 May 1996). *Applicants Who Missed Out on Tertiary Places*, Melbourne.

Airton, M (1995). Queensland Corrections: Policies, Practices and Practicalities, *Conference Proceedings*, Hobart, IFEPS.

Brooker, A (1996). *BEAT: A Bridging Education and Training Service*, Broadmeadows, Kangan Institute of TAFE.

Byrne, B (1995). Provision of Aboriginal Education in Correctional Centres – Central West NSW, *IFEPS Conference Proceedings*, Hobart.

Byrne, E (1991). *Unlocking Minds: From Retribution to Rehabilitation*, Queensland, University of Queensland.

Carmichael, L (Chair) (1992). *The Australian Vocational Certificate Training System: Report*, Canberra, National Board of Employment, Education and Training.

Collins, M K (Chair) (1984). *Integration in Victorian Education: Report, Melbourne*, Education Department.

Corrections Industry Training Board (1993). *Corrections Industry Training Plan*, Melbourne, Office of Corrections.

Dawkins, J S, and Holding, AC (1987). *Skills for Australia*, Canberra, Australian Government Printing Service.

Deveson, I (Chair) (1992). *Taskforce on Pathways in Education and Training: Report*, Melbourne, Department of School Education.

Dwyer, P (1995). Pathways in Post-Compulsory Education – From Metaphor to Practice, *Australian Journal of Education*, 39, 2: 146 162.

Fairman, B, and Wilson, R (1995). Community/ TAFE Partnerships in Education and Training, *Conference Proceedings*, Hobart, IFEPS.

Finn, B (Chair) (1991). *Young Peoples' Participation in Post-Compulsory Education and Training*, Canberra, Australian Government Printing Service.

Halstead, B, and Edwards, A (1992). *Keeping Them In and Keeping Them Out: Education and Training Programs Available to Prisoners and Ex-Prisoners in Australia*, Canberra, Australian Institute of Criminology.

House of Representatives Standing Committee on Aboriginal and Torres Strait Islander Affairs (1994). *Justice Under Scrutiny: Report of the Inquiry into the Implementation by Governments of the Recommendations of the Royal Commission into Aboriginal Deaths in Custody*, Canberra, Parliament of Australia.

International Taskforce on Indigenous Rights in Education (1993). *The Coolangatta Statement*, Woollongong, World Indigenous Peoples' Conference.

Kirby, P (Chair) (1985). *Committee of Inquiry into Labour Market Programs: Report*, Canberra, Australian Government Printing Service.

Mayer, E (Chair) (1992). *Employment-Related Key Competencies: A Proposal for Consultation*, Melbourne, Author.

Meatheringham, B (1995). Development of Offender Services in South Australia, *Conference Proceedings*, Hobart, IFEPS.

Noad, B (1995). Overview of Policies, Practices and Current Provision of Education and Training for Inmates in NSW Correctional Centres, *Conference Proceedings*, Hobart, IFEPS.

Roberts, J and Wilmott, T (1994). Where Do Penal Systems Begin and End for Offenders? Recent Developments in Community-Based Corrections, *IFEPS Conference Proceedings*, Melbourne, IFEPS.

Royal Commission (1991) *Aboriginal Deaths in Custody: Report*, Canberra, Australian Government Printing Service.

Semmens, R (1988). *Vocational Training in a Prison Environment: Report*, Melbourne, State Training Board.

Semmens, R (1991). *Program Evaluation at Barwon Prison, Canberra*, Australian Institute of Criminology.

Semmens, R (1992). Employment, Education and Training Opportunities for Prisoners and Ex-Prisoners, *Commissioned Report No. 17*, Canberra, National Board of Employment, Education and Training.

Semmens, R (1994). The Case for a National Agenda for Employment, Education and Training of Offenders, *IFEPS Conference Proceedings, Melbourne*, IFEPS.

Semmens, R (1996). *Evaluation of Vocational Training at Fairlea Women's Prison*, University of Melbourne.

Senate Standing Committee on Employment, Education and Training (1991). *Come In Cinderella: The Emergence of Adult and Community Education*, Canberra, Senate.

Sirr, P (ed) (1992). The Way Out: The Role of Employment, Education and Training for Offenders in the Criminal Justice Systems, *Conference Proceedings,* Perth, Outcare.

Tierney, J (Chair) (1996). *Inquiry Into Education and Training in Correctional Facilities: Report*, Canberra, Senate Employment, Education and Training References Committee.

Van Groningen, J (1995). The Impact of Privatisation on the Delivery of Vocational Education and Training Programs to the Corrections System in Victoria, *Conference Proceedings*, Hobart, IFEPS.

Wilson, R, and Penaluna, K (1995) Training Pathways in Victorian Prisons: Results to Date, *Conference Proceedings*, Hobart, IFEPS.

Chapter Two

Policy, praxis and rehabilitation: prison education in Canada 1945–1995

Stephen Duguid, Simon Fraser University, Vancouver, BC

One can at times talk about education abstracted from society, politics and even from schools, or at least pretend to, but in the field of prison education the context is pervasive. The prison classroom is embedded within the confines of a prison system that is at once authoritarian and fiercely independent within its walls, fences and imposing mandate. Yet at the same time it is always vulnerable to shifts in public policy as government responds to public feelings about crime, safety and correction. Never has this schizophrenic position of the prison – at once powerful and vulnerable – been more evident than in recent years as it has been faced with a trilogy of pressures: a politically-inspired war on drugs, a culturally-driven prosecution of sexual deviance, and an often hysterical popular fear of violent crime. These pressures, continental if not global in extent, have buffeted the prison or corrections enterprise along with its partners in law enforcement and the judiciary, and prison education has had to go along for the ride.

The 'politics of crime and corrections', therefore, forms the essential context for this examination of prison education in Canada. Stepping back even further, this context cannot be fully understood separately from the United States experience, there being such powerful cultural affinities between that country and Canada, some elective and some manipulated. These affinities include interlocking corrections and academic organisations, strong personal connections amongst the relevant 'experts' and the similarity of the educational systems of the two countries. Locked in their shared geography, Canada and the United States also share many social trends, legal and illegal, and even share some criminals.

There are, of course, important distinctions between the Canadian and American context which make the former sufficiently distinct to warrant separate study. Unlike the United States, the dominant correctional system in Canada is a national one, the Correctional Service of Canada (CSC). In Canada, individuals convicted of any crime that brings with it a sentence of two years or more are automatically sent to a federal prison, provincial prison systems being responsible for all shorter sentences. Likewise, the much lower level of violence, and the different ethnic composition of Canada, result in a quite different range of offences, sentences, punishments and prisoner population.

Education is one enterprise amongst many within this corrections context, sharing resources and roles with vocational training, employment, institutional services, counselling and various psychological/medical programmes and interventions and, of course, security. Like many of these activities, education can be viewed as rehabilitative, as job training, as a component of prison management, or as merely a luxury tolerated only when convenient. It can also expand and contract in scope, ranging from basic literacy and numeracy skills to university graduation. The relative position of education in the hierarchy of activities that take place within the prison shifts over time and the determinant to those shifts has less to do with educational theory than with correctional theory and public policy.

The corrections context 1996

The Canadian public is convinced that crime is increasing, that they are more subject to violence than ever before and that this is in part the result of lax penal policy, particularly the system of parole. Criminologists from across Canada generally disagree, insisting that 'The country is not getting more violent' (Elliott Leyton, Memorial University, Newfoundland); 'Canadians are scaring themselves to death over crime [but] it is not getting worse' (John Ekstedt, Simon Fraser University, British Columbia). The police, on the other hand, tend to support the public on this issue. The Head of the Royal Canadian Mounted Police (RCMP) Serious Crime Division has stated, 'I think the public perception is dead on'.[1] There does seem to be some truth to both sides, in that while murder rates (the standard measure of crime rates) in Canada are falling, burglary and car theft are increasing, spousal abuse and sexual assault cases are more readily reported (and deemed particularly newsworthy by the media) and, as a spillover from the United States, concern for drug-related crime remains high.[2] Meanwhile, reflecting reduced resources for police, arrest rates are down.[3]

In responding to public pressure and to actual issues of public safety, governments in North America have, as we hear constantly, 'gotten tough on crime'. But this toughness seldom manifests itself in crime prevention or even apprehension, but rather in the bureaucratically more convenient and publicly more satisfying realm of punishment: in the courts and in the prisons. Thus in the United States a 'no frills for prisons' section was added to the Republican's 1994 Take Back Our Streets Act, the State of Alabama brought back the chain gang, capital punishment has spread and prisons continued to overflow with new inmates. Education suffered accordingly, the Governor of Massachusetts being not atypical in calling for prisons to be a ' . . . tour through the circles of hell . . . where prisoners should learn only the joys of busting rocks' (Worth,

1995: 38). In a dramatic reversal of recent trends in prison education, financial aid for post-secondary education for prisoners (Pell Grants) was cancelled, funding was reduced across the board for literacy and basic education, and prisoners increasingly were left to learn on their own by independent study.

The parallel responses in Canada were predictably much more muted and moderate. Alberta, for instance, flirted with chain gangs but backed off after polling suggested Albertans were worried the programme would have focused too much on punishment and not enough on rehabilitation. Still, some education programmes in prisons were cancelled, funds were reduced and sentencing grew more punitive.

The two developments that have come to characterise this new toughness on crime are the Three Strikes phenomenon and the appearance of military-style Boot Camps for young offenders. The Three Strikes law made its first appearance in California and was largely the accomplishment of one man, Mike Reynolds, whose daughter Polly Klaas had been kidnapped and murdered in 1993.[4] The father's demand that 'something be done' unleashed a ' . . . political tidal wave' that quickly spread across a continent and resulted in similar laws in many other states. While Canada has so far avoided this somewhat draconian option, it has followed suit indirectly by increasing usage of the Dangerous Offender legislation passed in 1977, legislation which effectively denies parole to prisoners so designated.[5] In response to specific crimes there have been several high-profile attempts by citizen groups in several provinces, British Columbia and Ontario in particular, to pressurise the Canadian government to expand this legislation further, to limit or eliminate parole and to introduce a Three Strikes policy.

Three Strikes, of course, is not effective in preventing or deterring crime in that it locks up the wrong people, inflicting a great deal of pain on offenders who have committed relatively minor offences. But it is effective in the political sense in that governments are seen to be doing something about crime. Boot Camps are another classic example of this paradox. By 1994 there were 79 Boot Camp Programmes in the United States and in 1995 they were opening in Ontario, in Alberta and even in England, despite being notoriously expensive and having proved to have no appreciable impact upon the future criminal activities of their graduates. Where there was an impact, researchers indicated that it was likely due to the more traditional education and counselling programmes included in the Camp, rather than to the military regime employed.[6] Still, the media images of uniformed men disciplining undisciplined youth seemed to mesh with common sense notions of corrections.

In Canada the issue of sex offenders has become a particularly salient feature of the highly-charged context in which both corrections and prison education must exist. Even more than in the United States, where sexual offenders are often treated as 'regular prisoners', prisoners in Canada have always treated their sex offending colleagues as pariahs and now the public has joined them with a vengeance.[7] In 1988, the CSC had four sex offender programmes with an annual capacity of 200 inmates. In 1995, the CSC claims to have had about 70 programmes treating about 2,100 sex offenders. The sex offender population has ' . . . continued to grow rapidly and disproportionately to the total non-sex offender population . . . ', increasing by 40 per cent from 1990 to 1995, currently comprising 24 per cent of the incarcerated individuals within the CSC (Motiuk and Belcourt, 1996). Accompanying this new fixation on sexual offences (including sexual assault, incest, paedophilia) is the belief that while some are incurable psychopaths, most can be treated by focussing on issues such as anger, lack of social skills and skewed thinking patterns. As will become evident, in Canada this linkage between deviance and thinking skills and patterns is a central feature of current correctional theory and has had an important impact on prison education.

As a backdrop to all these developments – get-tough policies, Three Strikes, Boot Camps and mandatory detention – lie the prognostications of the social demographers, that in the 21st century we will be faced with a new generation of ' . . . super-predators . . . a new variety of young criminal who has no adults in his life and no apparent capacity for remorse' (Worth, 1995). The American Attorney General Janet Reno has warned that by 2010 there could be as many as a quarter of a million juveniles aged 6–17 arrested for violent crimes in the United States and many are talking in terms of an emerging new 'criminal class' which will cause widespread disorder in cities and an increasing number of small-scale, vicious crimes. Anticipating this theme, the popular media consistently play up youth crime, focussing in particular on the more spectacular cases.

This context of crisis occurs, of course, in the midst of massive cuts in government spending on corrections, cutbacks in prison treatment programmes, overcrowding within prisons, and an increasing trend toward privatisation within corrections. Amidst this maelstrom of shrinking resources, employment insecurity, public demands for effectiveness, government demands for account-ability, prisoner demands for fair treatment, and the demands of victims for retribution, there remains the teacher, the classroom, the student, the cur-riculum and the pedagogy of prison education, or correctional education as it is often called in North America. To understand where prison education sits now in corrections and how it may respond to this context, we have firstly to examine its historical track through the shifting paradigms of modern cor-rectional theory.

The medical model: 1945–1975

Education has been a major component of prisons and corrections since the 18th century enlightenment. Borrowing Plato's idea that crime can only flow from ignorance, prison workers experimented with various educational approaches with their charges, ranging from intense Bible reading, to equally intense self-reflection. From the mid–19th century, as society became more urbanised, illiteracy came to be seen as the major cause of criminal activity. Harvey Graff has outlined in great detail how ' . . . illiteracy itself was raised to a causal factor . . . along with ignorance . . .' The great Canadian educator Egerton Ryerson embraced the idea of general education as the ' . . . most effectual prevention of pauperism, and its natural companions, misery and vice . . . [and that] pauperism and crime prevail in proportion to the absence of education amongst the labouring classes' (Graff, 1979: 235). Thus was constructed what Graff refers to as the 'rhetorical house' which explained criminality and, quite logically, placed education at the centre of the prison's mission.

This was perhaps the first example of the many perils prison educators and reformers have faced as a result of promising more than could reasonably be delivered. As literacy rates rose in North America throughout the 19th and early 20th centuries, among the 'labouring classes' and even within prisons, crime continued to increase and released prisoners continued to recidivate. Educators responded to this paradox (for them) by arguing that they just were not doing enough, that a more inclusive education was needed, or that a new pedagogy might be more effective. But the correctional enterprise began to shift from the 1930s toward first biological and then psychological explanations for criminal behaviour. These early attempts to utilise science to explain deviance were quite crude, including as they did phrenology, heredity studies and crude attempts at criminal typologies. But they set the pace for a much more sophisticated post-war approach, called the Medical Model, an approach to corrections, built upon the social sciences that had come to such prominence during the Second World War.

The Medical Model was exactly that, an approach to criminal behaviour that saw it as an illness, the specific causes of which could be diagnosed and prescribed for. How else, indeed, in the Panglossian best of all possible worlds of post-war modernity, could one explain the persistent refusal of some to pursue the lawful path? Thus it was concluded that:

> . . . imprisonment and punishment do not present themselves as the proper methods of dealing with criminals. We have to treat them physically as sick people, which in every respect they are . . . It is the hope of the more progressive elements in psychopathology and criminology that the guard and jailer will be replaced by the nurse and the judge by the psychiatrist . . . (Karpman, 1949 in Cressey, 1960: 88).

It is important that we fix this model firmly in mind if current flirtations with a 'new medical model' are to be understood and appreciated. Correctional policy shifted dramatically in the 1950s toward the objective of ' . . . reformation through individualized treatment' (Cressey, 1960: 86). Educational activities, along with industries one of the mainstays of the prison regime, were now replaced or subsumed by programmes and treatments were aimed more directly at altering personalities. The actual words used by proponents of the Model are important, especially reformation, treatment, and altering personalities. This was no easy transformation and many in the prisons, staff and prisoners, resisted these new ideas, provoking the new experts to complain that more had to be done, that the prisons had to become hospitals with a ' . . . harmony of purpose [and] all employees will be accepting of the inmates as troubled persons in need of treatment (Fenton, 1956: 28).'[8]

What happened to prison education during this era? The time-honoured mandate to provide basic literacy and numeracy continued, but given the more grandiose objectives of the era a more striking response from educators was required. Indeed, within the traditional sectors of education, standards seemed to slip with widespread use of inmate teachers, inadequate books and equipment and poor standards (Peretti, 1969). Where prison education grew during this era was at the higher end of the spectrum, in college and university programmes and in the educational components of other treatment programmes. The first in-person college programme in North America began in 1957, operated by Southern Illinois University at Menard Prison. Delyte Morris, President of the University, described its mission in language taken directly from the spirit and substance of the Medical Model:

Such academic education in prison is supposed to advance rehabilitation. Through improved skills in communication, the offender presumably will be able to reveal and express underlying misunderstandings and conflicts which have caused his deviant behavior. The prisoner student will be able to comprehend more fully his personal problems and his relationships with other persons . . . Through better understanding of government and society, he will be moved toward responsible citizenship (Irwin, 1973: 10).

This carefully-worded mission statement combines some quite traditional educational objectives such as citizenship with important linkages to the reformational dimension of the new correctional agenda. As such, it remains a clear and succinct statement of the position of prison education programmes within a correctional system dedicated to reformation and rehabilitation.

It did not take long for the Illinois example to spread. By 1966 the University of California at Berkeley had a full-time accredited programme at San Quentin and within three years over 80 American colleges and universities were offering courses in prisons. In 1971, the US Office of Economic Opportunity began to fund the Newgate Programmes, university degree programmes combining education with therapeutic counselling and post-release support. With these Newgate Programmes education in prison began to march in step with the Medical Model, focussing as much on counselling and community reintegration as on offering education programmes.

In Canada, this development had by 1974 resulted in at least three major post-secondary programmes. The University of Manitoba was offering courses leading to a BA degree at Stoney Mountain Penitentiary; Queen's University in Kingston, Ontario began offering a small number of courses in several local federal prisons; and the University of Victoria had started its programme at the BC Penitentiary and at Matsqui Prison. Several community colleges soon took on prison education contracts in a number of institutions and there were signs that similar moves were going to take place in Quebec. Of this group, the University of Victoria's came the closest to matching the Newgate model, in this case linking the offering of courses with improvements in the moral and cognitive reasoning of prisoner-students. In part because of this willingness to at least consider being linked with the correctional agenda, the BC programme grew to be the largest and longest-lasting such experiment in Canada, being finally abandoned by the Federal Government only in 1993.

Despite these flirtations with a truly 'correctional' view of education, no major university programme in the United States or Canada in the 1970s joined completely with the Medical Model. The relationships established between post-secondary prison education programmes and the therapeutic treatment programmes were forced, or simply convenient, but never a matter of free choice. Indeed, by the mid-1970s the therapists had begun to stretch their credibility, especially with statements like the following from James McConnell, a Psychology Professor at the University of Michigan:

> I believe the day has come when we can combine sensory deprivation with drugs, hypnosis, and astute manipulation of reward and punishment to gain almost absolute control over an individual's behavior . . . We'd assume that a felony was clear evidence that the criminal had somehow acquired full-blown social neurosis and needed to be cured, not punished. We'd send him to a rehabilitation center where he'd undergo positive brainwashing . . . We'd probably have to restructure his entire personality (Trotter and Warren, 1974:180).

The professors and the experts had promised a lot since the heady days of the post-war era and they had been given a virtual free hand within much of the correctional system in North America. Special therapeutic prisons had been built, such as Matsqui Prison in British Columbia; the new language of rehabilitation had transformed convicts into inmates and residents; and the indeterminate sentence had filled the prisons and shifted power from courts to corrections. But had they delivered the goods?

The rejection of rehabilitation: 1974–1977

The 25-year reign of the Medical Model was brought to an end in virtually a matter of months in 1974, thanks to the publication of two very influential reviews of corrections, *The Future of Imprisonment* by Norval Morris and 'What

Works? Questions and Answers about Prison Reform' by Robert Martinson. There were two arguments being explicitly made in the texts, one empirical and the other philosophical. Martinson and his colleagues had surveyed over 200 studies of prison rehabilitation programmes and reported that the results ' . . . give us very little reason to hope that we have in fact found a sure way of reducing recidivism through rehabilitation'. This alone might have been deflating but not necessarily fatal to the rehabilitation project, since only the most foolhardy had claimed a *sure cure* for crime. The attack, however, was aimed in fact at the psychological paradigm itself, the idea that the origins of crime reside in the offender rather than in the offender's relations with society. Thus, Martinson continued:

> *Our present treatment programmes are based on a theory of crime as a disease —*
> *that is to say, as something foreign and abnormal in the individual which can*
> *presumably be cured. This theory may well be flawed, in that it overlooks — indeed*
> *denies — both the normality of crime in society and the personal normality of a very*
> *large proportion of offenders, criminals who are merely responding to the facts and*
> *conditions of our society (Martinson, 1974: 49).*

If the empirical argument that treatment programmes just were not effective enough to warrant their cost, either in money or in the human costs implicit in the extended prison stays of prisoners awaiting treatment and cure, the philosophical argument pointed the way toward an alternative. According to Morris, treatment, including education, could not work if it was coerced and he thus called for voluntary programmes. Morris and others were concerned that prisons as constituted were not only ineffectual, but also ' . . . made imprisonment seem legitimate and desirable . . . Fostering the illusion that inmates were locked up for their own good . . . ' (Rothman, 1994: 35). Martinson called for massive 'decarceration' for low-risk offenders and the containing of high-risk offenders in prisons which are nothing more (and aim to be nothing more) than custodial institutions. Both texts helped convince people in corrections of an essential contradiction at the heart of the Medical Model, namely that ' . . . a prison can't set itself up as an agent for helping an individual (rehabilitation) when its reason for existing is to do violence (by robbing him of his freedom)' (Holden, 1975: 816).

The following by a prisoner at the State Prison of Southern Michigan testifies to the centrality of Morris' point about the counselling/rehabilitation/treatment model:

> *From my point of view, the entire counselling-treatment program is a game, the*
> *rules of which I must try to learn in order to placate the prison officials and*
> *manipulate the parole board at my parole hearing. I have to serve my time, but in*
> *addition, I must also prove that the counsellor has been successful and that I am*
> *rehabilitated and ready for parole (Furtado and Johnson, 1980: 252).*

This insight proved particularly difficult for corrections to ignore while at the same time being distinctly unpalatable in that it restricted the roles possible for corrections professionals. If it were true that prisoners do not, by and large, feel sick or deviant – lawbreakers yes, but not sick – and that part of being a lawbreaker is a central dynamic of competition and disdain/hatred for lawkeepers, whether police or corrections, then it becomes a direct attack on the pride of the prisoner to expect him to acknowledge being cured of an imagined illness by a doctor for whom he has no respect.

The consequences of this attack were swift in coming. In Canada the Law Reform Commission in its 1975 paper *'Imprisonment and Release'* rejected rehabilitation as a rationale for sentencing and releasing decisions and in the 1977 discussion paper *'The Role of Federal Corrections in Canada'* it was suggested that an offender should never be sent to prison for the purpose of receiving treatment (Nuffield, 1982). Norman Carlson, the Director of the US Bureau of Prisons, said in 1976 that ' . . . the idea that rehabilitation is the sole purpose of prison is being discarded as unrealistic . . . Most of us in the field of criminal justice are now willing to admit that we don't know how to change offenders when they have no desire to change themselves.'[9] Later that year, the Canadian Solicitor General agreed that the claims that corrections can somehow manage to change the lifestyle of the offender are ' . . . unrealistic, unsubstantiated and unattainable . . . [and] . . . in the future, instead of trying to prescribe appropriate treatment to rehabilitate offenders, the correction system will expect prisoners to make use of available opportunities to earn their way out' (Fox, 1976).

New paradigms began to multiply and fill the void created by the destruction of the Medical Model. The Just Desserts/Retribution/Justice model was an early favourite. It called for shorter, fewer, but more certain sentences and sentences related directly to the crime, independent of the needs or personal history of the offender. Still to come were the Opportunities Model, Humane Containment and Selective Incapacitation. What was common to them all was the strategic withdrawal of corrections itself from the realm of treatment and even, in many cases, from the realm of programming in prisons *per se*, leaving room for educational institutions, amongst others, to expand their role in corrections. And the timing could not have been better. In Canada, the several universities and colleges mentioned above were new to the field and while some had edged close to heralding education as 'treatment', none had been around long enough to be identified strongly with the Medical Model. The other educational activities in Canadian prisons – secondary or high school education, adult basic education and vocational training – had suffered for so long in the shadow of their prestigious treatment cousins that they too emerged in the mid-1970s as important activities in prisons suddenly devoid of once-popular programmes. Nothing could have been more symbolic of this reversal of roles than the 1976 movement of the University Programme at Matsqui

Institution from a decrepit classroom adjacent to a busy walkway to a stand-alone building that only a year before had been the site of a therapeutic drug treatment programme and a transcendental meditation group.

The opportunities model: 1977–1987

Simply containing people, one of the possible outcomes of the rejection of rehabilitation, proved difficult for correctional professionals to accept. Like other professionals, people in corrections needed to feel productive, to be more than hospice workers or keepers. Besides, they knew from direct experience that many programmes, treatment or otherwise, did *work* in that they were often decisive in changing a prisoner's life. After all, Martinson's research only demonstrated that there was no *sure* success, no programme that worked at all times on all cases. The fact that governments chose to interpret Martinson as saying that literally 'nothing works' was as much a fiscal response and a pandering to public cynicism as it was a genuine response to the dilemma posed by high rates of recidivism. Martinson's anecdotal reference to benign neglect being as 'effective' as treatment was music to the ears of government accountants looking for money to save.

The Opportunities Model came complete with a magic word: choice. And the prisoner's right to choose was to become the key to correctional theory during this decade. William Outerbridge, Chairman of the National Parole Board at the time, set the theme in an interview in 1977:

> The obscenity of prison is very clearly this fact: a criminal is viewed as a man who can make choices and, out of all the available alternatives, chose to commit an offense. When we put him in prison we take away every opportunity of choice he has and then expect him to be able to make the right choices after he's been released. [10]

This notion of choice and its linkage with citizenship and making better choices after release was to become linked to the idea of development and through that, to become an integral component of the justification for a focus on education in Canadian prisons. The CSC itself rejected the label 'treatment', preferring to call programmes offered in their institutions as ' . . . offender development programs provided to assist offenders in developing their personal resources, their relationships with others, their skills and abilities, and their post-release situations' (CSC Orientation Manual, 1987). The continued interest in post-release lives signalled a lingering hope or faith in the rehabilitative ideal and there was clearly the assumption that participation in programmes, albeit voluntary, should lead to reductions in recidivism.

This continued eye cast on the issue of recidivism, more so in Canada than in the US or England, reflected in part the distance many in Canada felt from Martinson's pessimism and the much more humane and progressive conditions within Canadian prisons, leaving more room it seemed for positive custodial outcomes. Nonetheless, within the education providers in Canadian prisons this ambivalence resulted in some tensions. The University of Victoria post-secondary programme under the direction of Professor Douglas Ayers had been more proactive from its inception in making claims for reductions in recidivism. Research was on-going; follow-up studies were forthcoming; and as the programme expanded to more British Columbia prisons and took in more students, its claims for effectiveness grew more contentious. A parallel programme in Quebec, started by Professor Lucien Morin, was on a similar track, while post-secondary programmes in Ontario and Manitoba rejected this path, preferring to make the case for education without any necessary link to operational outcomes.

Within the educational branch of the CSC there remained a key group of educators in top management positions with a keen interest in refuting Martinson and demonstrating that education at least did work. A variety of initiatives were funded during these years, including a programme based on the work of Israeli psychologist and educator Reuven Feuerstein which focused on cognitive re-structuring. Programmes in teaching critical thinking were funded, linking them with the highschool-level education classes. Research was also conducted into the theory that education would lead to higher stages of moral development, based on the work of Lawrence Kohlberg at Harvard and his colleague Peter Scharf, then at the University of California. Briefly, and reminiscent of the theories of the 1960s, there was interest in the notion of the criminal personality then being written about by Yochelson and Samenow based at St Elizabeth's Hospital in Washington, DC.

From all these disparate but still connected initiatives and projects, there began to emerge what Thom Gehring was to call a 'Canadian Correctional Education Paradigm', consisting of five components: cognitive instruction (critical thinking); participative decision-making (choice); moral education; criminal personality; and focus on the humanities (Gehring, 1988: 13).

Gehring's construction suffered from a somewhat too close contact with the University of Victoria (later Simon Fraser University) Programme, but still there was some logic to his paradigm. While educators like Ayers and his counterparts in the CSC were talking about cognitive and moral development in a somewhat general way, Robert Ross and his student Elizabeth Fabiano at the University of Ottawa were working on a full-scale intervention programme designed for inmates, that zeroed in almost exclusively on cognitive development, or changing thinking patterns. Ross, the real force behind what was to become in the 1990s the CSC's flagship Cognitive Skills Programme, had begun thinking about this issue in the late 1970s and published his most complete exposition of the theory in *Time to Think: A Cognitive Model of Delinquency Prevention and Offender Rehabilitation* in 1985. Ross looked to the University Programme in British Columbia as a classic example of cognitive development in operation:

> *UVic challenged educationalists to de-emphasize the three Rs and to focus on cognitive restructuring, moral development, and problem solving in the interpersonal and social skills necessary for the prisoner to function prosocially in society. These goals were taught in undergraduate humanities courses, a direct but subtle method of teaching social cognitive skills. Professors, employing small groups and Socratic dialogue, served as role models and presented information not as a 'treatment' of personal deficits, but for the purposes of working toward a university degree. This latter strategy was important, as many of the participants were older high-risk offenders with long and serious criminal histories, who might resent a traditional authoritarian approach (Gendreau and Ross, 1987: 365).*

This version of the university programme in British Columbia would have clashed head-on with the perspective of most of the teaching staff in the programme, few of whom saw themselves as pursuing 'social cognitive skills' or 'cognitive restructuring'. Neither was their primary ambition to enable prisoner-students to 'function prosocially in society'. While many would have dismissed these objectives out of hand and insisted that they were simply teaching history, psychology or anthropology, others at least acknowledged the complexity of the situation. One of the staff summed up the slippery slope between education and treatment that needed negotiating in the following way:

> *Within the parameters of these two goals there are two potential errors: the error of academic degeneration and the error of academic insularity. The goals of the program could be thwarted by sacrificing academic quality, such that the prisoners dismiss the program as another social therapy exercise, or the program and faculty could remain aloof from the social reality of prison and prisoner and fail to provide sufficient support for the development of a cohesive, identifiable scholastic community of prisoners. (Knights, 1982).*

The third component of Gehring's Canadian paradigm, democratic decision-making, was an integral part of the university experience in British Columbia and no doubt in other post-secondary programmes. Staffed largely by younger academics who had come up through the university turmoil of the 1970s, student-centred teaching, participatory seminars and democratic management were part of the ethos of the time – a happy coincidence given the focus on choice so central to the Opportunities Model (Duguid, 1987).

This aspect of prison education also allowed for a closer alignment with one of the central pillars of adult education, namely that students must be active participants in the education process. Nonetheless, there remained a central conflict between prison education and adult education in that whether in the Basic Education, High School or Higher Education programmes, the curriculum was largely set independently of the perceived learning needs of the students. Thus while many prisoner-students wanted business and media courses, or language instruction in Spanish or computer programming courses, their choices were generally constrained not only by limited resources, but by what the providers anticipated would best assist them in their post-release lives. In some cases this directive, top-down approach meant that the courses or programmes available were limited by the assumption of many in Corrections that base level employment was all that could be expected from these men, hence the focus on literacy, numeracy and trades training. In other cases, the university programme in BC for example, it meant that courses in the humanities were mandatory since these were seen as the most effective means of triggering cognitive and moral development. Whatever it promised, then, the Opportunities Model in fact remained quite directive in terms of the actual choices offered.

The fourth component of Gehring's Canadian paradigm, the focus on something called a 'criminal personality', was the most controversial and in many ways the most influential. It has led to some alarming research and speculations about psychopathy, sexual predators, and professional criminals. Applied to the education of prisoners during this period, it tended to focus on the idea of deficits, that prisoner-students were unique compared with other adult learners in the particular range of cognitive deficits that they displayed.

Carol LaBar and Ian Wright, researchers in the teaching of critical thinking, came up with a list of seven deficiencies common to a great many prisoner-students. According to them, prisoners will:

- have difficulty deferring gratification;
- tend not to be disposed to imagine themselves in the situation of another person;
- tend not to see the point of the concept of obligation;
- tend not to trust other people;
- tend not to gather relevant information and weigh the pros and cons of a course of action before deciding on it. They think they have all the information they need;
- tend to be unwilling to suspend judgment on persons and courses of action; and
- tend to be close-minded. They will not listen to evidence which contradicts what they already believe (LaBar *et al*: 266).

While there are always difficulties with typologies like this, for those with direct experience in the prisons the characteristics matched their experience in too many ways to be ignored. If there was rough common ground, then, amongst educators in prisons concerned with the learning characteristics and even needs of the students, there remained considerable disagreement about how these should be addressed in the classroom.

Gehring's final component, the focus on the humanities, was favoured by one side in this debate, the side which called for an indirect approach to the problem. By utilising traditional academic subject matter, particularly a problem-oriented humanities curriculum, it was presumed that the student would be either: affected; developed and/or changed without him being fully aware of the process. The others involved in the debate saw this approach as potentially ineffectual and wasteful of time and resources, preferring a much more direct attack on the problem via programmes in critical thinking or cognitive restructuring. An uneasy tension existed between these two approaches, both existing *within* the educational community and operating in the prisons through staff responsible for inmate programmes. In many prisons, programmes epitomising these two approaches existed side by side, often drawing on the same students, sometimes in competition, and always forced to share increasingly scarce resources. It was, one could surmise, the inability of these two strains to find common ground in the late 1980s that contributed to the eventual shift within the CSC to a focus on the direct programming for cognitive skills independent of education units.

Shifting paradigms: the emergence of cognitive skills

The lack of interest within corrections in prison programming during the decade 1975–1985, which was the direct outcome of the demoralisation triggered by the 'nothing works' debate, had created a vacuum quickly filled by other professionals from outside corrections. In Canada three distinct but interrelated groups took up the challenge of prison education and prisoner rehabilitation: college and university faculty teaching in secondary and post-secondary prison education programmes; adult educators interested in literacy, basic education and living skills; and university-based researchers and private consultants.

As the CSC gradually disbanded its internal research capability (after all, why do research when *nothing works*?) and began to retire its cohort of in-house teachers – in effect beginning the process of privatisation – educational research and practice in the prisons was carried on by contracts with individuals and institutions from these three groups. The effect of this shift was to bring the subject of prison education and prisoner rehabilitation into a much wider discourse community. It was a community that included national and international organisations such as the Correctional Education Association, the International Council for Adult Education and the various organisations associated with the study of criminology.

The first two of these groups, who might best be characterised respectively as teacher-oriented and social change-oriented, achieved the most public prominence during this era. The post-secondary 'stream' in Canadian prison education, led during this period by staff from the university programme in British Columbia, achieved particular prominence within the then US-based Correctional Education Association (CEA) and played an important role in the creation of the European Prison Education Association (EPEA). The impact of this group on prison education generally reached its climax in 1990 when Simon Fraser University hosted the International CEA Conference in Vancouver, attended by over 800 delegates from some 30 countries. The adult educators achieved a similar degree of success within the world of corrections via their work on literacy and life skills programming. In 1987, the CSC hosted a major conference in Ottawa on Offender Literacy and announced a major shift of resources to this area of prisoner education. It was the third group, however, which proved to be the most potent in terms of its impact on prison education in Canada. By the early 1990s, its work on Cognitive Living Skills and theories on offender rehabilitation had easily eclipsed the accomplishments of the others.

The triumph of the Cognitive Skills initiative in Canada (and its rapid spread to other correctional jurisdictions) was a signal that, in Canada at least, the era of *nothing works* was over, that the passive policy of the Opportunities Model was out, and that a New Medical Model – firmly in the hands of professional correctional staff and their research consultants – was in. How did this happen? Where did this new faith in treatment come from? And what was its impact on prison education?

In 1985 a report surfaced within the CSC entitled 'Review of Offender Support Programs', the so-called Sawatsky Report, which helped set this process in motion. In the language of the report one can hear the early acceptance of what subsequently came to be known as criminogenic factors, predispositions within the offender which if left untouched would lead to further deviance. More importantly, the Report sounded the death knell for the Opportunities Model, the essential first step if corrections was going to assume a more proactive role in prison programming:

> The 'opportunities model' is . . . a primary contributor to the instability [in correctional programming]. Because this model assumes the offender to be responsible, the staff have, regrettably, all too often seen their responsibility as being only to ensure that the offender is afforded program opportunities of his choice. The result of this orientation has seemingly created a 'window-shopping mentality' where inmates 'wander' or 'drift' in and out of programs without addressing key areas of need or seeing a particular program through to its completion (Sawatsky, 1985:14).

The language used in even this brief excerpt from the Sawatsky Report is rich in meaning and interpretation. To 'wander' and 'drift' is an explicit critique of what others might see simply as individuals making choices. The fact that it is taken as a guarantee, that each inmate has 'key areas of need' and, unsaid but implicit, that these can be known and provided for by outsiders, bodes well for a new faith in treatment. And the assumption that programmes (which address needs) have 'completion' as a guarantee, re-opens the door to the indeterminate sentence, the insistence that release be linked to programme completion. Finally, and most importantly, there is the rejection of the adult education approach explicit in the Opportunities Model, in that prisoners are no longer to be assumed to be 'responsible'. Instead the path is open to the continued infantilisation of the prisoner, from decision-maker to victim of dispositions, chemicals or genes or a patient in need of therapy and cure.

One can also hear in the Sawatsky Report the beginning of the end for post-secondary education programmes in Canadian prisons. It is referred to in passing as perhaps useful to long-term and/or maximum security inmates ' . . . who seem to find it ego-gratifying . . .' and thus use it to ' . . . constructively occupy time . . . ', but while it is perceived by some staff to be a ' . . . nice program to have, it is not essential – not core and could be reduced if necessary' (Sawatsky, 1985: 34). This judgement stood uncontested within the CSC despite a 1979 study of recidivism from the BC post-secondary programme that shows remarkably high success rates. Robert Ross, in speaking about this study, noted that: 'Nowhere else in the literature can one find such impressive results with recidivistic adult offenders' (Ross, 1985: 89).

A number of forces were converging in the late 1980s which were to transform the approach of corrections to prisoner rehabilitation and, in the process, eviscerate the Correctional Education Paradigm that Gehring had seen maturing in Canada since the 1970s. We can summarise these forces as follows:

1) The growing demand on the part of the public that the government, particularly the justice system, be seen to be doing something about violent crime, with a particular focus on the problem of parolled prisoners recommitting crimes. This meant a shift toward either an American-style expansion of prisons and sentences or a renewed effort at rehabilitation;

2) The beginnings of massive public concern with issues of the national deficit, spending in general and the size of government, leading to annual reductions in the budgets of most government departments. Demands for greater efficiency became transformed into demands for accountability, which in turn were dependent on the ability to quantify results;

3) A shift in organisational policy within governments at both provincial and federal levels leading toward a more vigorous demand for accountability, both in fiscal and programmatic terms. This was accompanied in the case of prison education departments across Canada by a gradual replacement of professional educators by professional managers in key civil service positions, with the result that bureaucratic decision-making about prison education was no longer in the hands of educators.

The educational institutions, including universities, colleges and school districts, which now provided the bulk of education programming in prisons, faced equally strong fiscal pressures and found increasingly stringent contracts with the CSC to be no longer as attractive as they had been in earlier years. This led to on-going contract difficulties and the shift toward a further level of privatisation, namely the concluding of contracts to provide educational services between the CSC and private companies. These entrepreneurial companies were often led by former college or school district employees who managed to undercut the bids of their former employers by avoiding union or institutional agreements, reducing employee benefits or in some cases lowering wages. By utilising provincial or national accreditation systems, they were able to meet the CSC's basic education and training needs without being connected with an established educational institution or jurisdiction.

These three trends were accompanied by a crucial fourth development, the growing commitment within the CSC to take over the central programme areas within the prisons and to recommit to a rehabilitative model built around the Cognitive Skills Programme being constructed by university-based researchers supported by a newly-revived Research Division within the CSC. The Cognitive Skills approach had three primary attractions for the prison authorities.

First, it was 'directly rehabilitative' in its approach to rehabilitation:

The program focused on modifying the impulsive, egocentric, illogical and rigid thinking of offenders and on teaching them to stop and think before acting, to consider the consequences of their behaviour, to conceptualize alternative ways of responding to interpersonal problems and to consider the impact of their behaviour on other people. (Ross, Fabiano and Ewles, 1988:3–4).

Utilising eighty hours of lessons on topics such as critical thinking, assertiveness training, role-playing and social perspective taking, the Cognitive Skills Programme sought to ameliorate in a direct fashion the thinking errors and deficits that Ross and his colleagues had found to be at the root of criminal decision-making. This was seen as potentially much more efficient than, for instance, education's claim to accomplish much the same through a more indirect approach.

Second, the programme was designed to be taught completely by Correctional Service staff. Elizabeth Fabiano, who had shifted from Carleton University to a job with the CSC, was responsible for establishing a national training programme for CSC staff, complete with a cadre of trainers schooled directly by Ross and Fabiano and then sent out to the regions to establish Cognitive Skills programmes in each prison. This had the double effect of saving money by a more efficient utilisation of staff and at the same time raising the morale of staff by assigning them a more positive role within corrections. In a tour of several Cognitive Skills Programmes in 1993, Ian Benson from the English Prison Department noted that the programme was very costly in terms of utilisation of staff, but that this was tolerated because the programme was such a ' . . . morale booster for staff . . . They appeared to relish an enhanced role which gave them greater status, job satisfaction and perhaps promotion prospects' (Benson, 1993).

Third, the research into the effectiveness of prison programmes conducted by Donald Andrews and Robert Ross led to the recommendation that programming be focused on high-risk prisoners, that is, prisoners with a high potential for recidivism. Andrews had re-visited the Martinson terrain and concluded that at least 40 per cent of the 'better controlled' correctional treatment services had positive effects, suggesting that ' . . . some service programs are working with at least some offenders under some circumstances' (Andrews, 1990: 374). And the ones that were most effective were those that concentrated their efforts on high-risk inmates, leading Andrews to recommend that the 'risk principle' be one of the keys to correctional programming:

> *According to the risk principle, intensive controls and services are best reserved for higher risk cases, while lower risk cases are best assigned to lower levels of service and control. The principle suggests that higher levels of supervision may reduce the recidivism of higher risk probationers but will have no such effect on the recidivism of low risk cases. Indeed, the principle suggests that, at best, the assignment of low risk cases to intensive service is a waste of scarce resources. At worst, assignment to service may be criminogenic for low risk cases. (Andrews, 1986: 377).*

In addition to its promised effectiveness, this approach had obvious fiscal attractions for the CSC. More importantly for our purposes, such a policy decision had a dramatic impact on education programmes which might attempt to make some claim for rehabilitative potential since, by its very nature, a high school, university or other education programme could not restrict entry to only high-risk prisoner-students.

Throughout the 1980s there had been a serious research endeavour in the United States to identify the career criminal, the small percentage of offenders who were responsible for the great majority of crimes and who had high rates of recidivism. Since the *nothing works* research of the 1970s had shown that treatment was generally ineffective when spread over the entire inmate population, the response of those still wedded to the psychological explanation of criminal behaviour sought out the smaller group of the 'truly deviant' for whom treatment could be effective.[11] In Canada, this process was operationalised through the concept of criminogenic needs, identifying the specific deficits or errors that characterised the thinking, feeling and behaviour of this smaller group of high-risk offenders and designing specific treatment programmes to meet those needs. Andrews argued that 'appropriate treatment (ie, treatment that addressed these needs) would cut recidivism for this high-risk group by 50 per cent' (Andrews, 1990:385).

As the Cognitive Skills Programme was duly implemented across Canada, all correctional programmes including education were asked to justify themselves (ie, their budget) in terms of their contribution to meeting the criminogenic needs of the offender population. This might mean, for instance, explaining how an education programme addressed: anger management needs; addiction needs; family relations; violence; or sexual deviance needs. While literacy and social reintegration skills were also identified as criminogenic needs and were areas that education could address, they were generally much lower in priority than the more obvious needs linked to violence, drugs and sexual deviance. In 1993, the university programme in British Columbia fell victim to this process after over 20 years of successful operation and similar programmes across Canada fell by the wayside.

Coming full circle: the new medical model

What a change in 20 years! In 1976 the Solicitor General of Canada had stated that attempts to change the lifestyle of the prisoner were 'unrealistic, unsubstantiated and unattainable', while in 1994 a spokesman for the CSC confidently asserted that 'Reducing re-offending by changing offenders from criminal to law-abiding lifestyles is a central theme in corrections in Canada . . . the Canadian correctional system is predicated on the assumption that offenders can change from a criminal to a law-abiding life style . . .' (Cormier, 1994). CSC staff now talk openly of a 'rehabilitation model' that assumes that: offenders have needs that directly cause their criminal behaviour; that we can diagnose those needs accurately; that appropriate intervention is available; that intervention will reduce those needs; and that reduced need will diminish criminal behaviour (Stewart and Millson, 1995: 5).[12] This confidence is grounded almost exclusively in the Cognitive Skills Programme and related treatments that address specific criminogenic factors. Education, Vocational Training and Industries are minor players in the new rehabilitative prison, supporting treatment programmes and occupying the time of prisoners – especially those deemed to be non-high-risk or those deemed untreatable – but no longer seen as key to the achievement of the correctional system's primary objective of 'reducing re-offending'. As one can imagine, accompanying that diminished role is a diminution of resources, both fiscal and material. The correctional system was becoming highly charged with this new and vigorous mandate, staff were sent to training sessions and imbued with the optimistic rhetoric of rehabilitation and treatment, and anyone not *on side* was in danger of being marginalised. Education programmes and education staff were faced with the demand not only to believe in rehabilitation but to believe in a particular path to that end and to transform their educational efforts to contribute to that end. Even corrections staff who were sceptical pointed to the public mood about crime – the context we opened with – and argued that the system had to be seen to be acting aggressively.

This approach is not without its critics, of course, and three areas of the model are seen as being particularly vulnerable: the viability of the prediction of high risk offenders; the reality of being able to diagnose the needs of individual offenders; and the practical possibility of actually delivering on what is promised. The prediction of who amongst a given population are the high-risk offenders needing treatment is a risky proposition. This is especially the case since one of the operational implications of this policy is that if one so designated refuses treatment or shows no signs of being cured, then release becomes problematic. The difficulty is in the science of prediction which is claimed by most social scientists to be notoriously inaccurate, thereby undermining the possibility of assigning the truly appropriate treatment to specific inmates. Advocates of the model, of course, claim their prediction system is generally accurate, but this remains to be seen. The false positives issue remains a sticky moral dilemma for any intervention relying on prediction systems.[13]

The diagnostic issue is quite similar. The model depends on the accuracy of a series of instruments and judgements made concerning the specific criminogenic needs of each offender. Checklists are utilised and line staff in institutions across the country assess each inmate at the time of induction and in a case conference determine the offender's treatment needs. Many researchers doubt that sufficient information is available to undertake such an assessment and doubt the veracity of the data that is present. Nonetheless, once diagnosed, the inmate must proceed through the prescribed treatment to progress easily through the sentence, especially if he or she has been deemed a high-risk offender (a designation based on yet another prediction device).

Finally, there is considerable scepticism that the will or resources are available to deliver the goods. One critic insists that the model is hopelessly 'utopian' in its claims about provision of treatment, as well as being wrong-headed in its single-minded focus on treatment being linked to psychological speculations about the needs of individuals (Lab and Whitehead, 1990: 410).

It is, however, on the claim that 'reduced need will diminish criminal behaviour' that the cognitive skills programme like so many others in corrections will be judged. As of 1995, over 3,500 federal prisoners had completed the Cognitive Skills Program and 2,125 who had been released for a minimum of one year are the subjects of a recently published CSC-conducted follow-up study. Of these 2,125 men, 1,444 had successfully completed the Program, 379 were in a Control Group and 302 were Program drop-outs (Robinson, 1995). The 60-page report, complete with charts, tables, graphs and lengthy analyses has to admit, sadly for the fate of Cognitive Skills, that 44.5 per cent of the programme completers were re-admitted to prison within the year, compared to 50.1 per cent for the Control Group, a reduction of a mere 11.2 per cent in recidivism – not a significant result. Even more disturbing, when the group was analysed in terms of High-risk to re-offend vs. Low-risk to re-offend, the high-risk group showed 'little gain from the programme', the low-risk group in fact accounting for most of the programmes' success. This was despite the predictions by all concerned that high-risk prisoners would benefit most and the virtually unanimous opinion in Corrections that high-risk offenders were the primary concern.

Interestingly, in a parallel follow-up study of some 650 prisoner-students from the now-defunct post-secondary programme in British Columbia, quite different results have recently been obtained (Duguid, 1996). Using an even more elaborate version of the risk prediction device used by Robinson (The Statistical Information on Recidivism SIR), approximately 80 per cent of the total group of 650 successfully completed three years of release (not just the one year in the Cognitive Skills study) and of the 117 men in the highest recidivism risk category – in which only one out three, or 33 per cent, is predicted to avoid recidivism – 57 per cent were successes after three years.[14] While virtually all the men in the lowest risk category (in which four out of five, or 80 per cent, are predicted not to re-offend) were in fact successful in this group of students, the truly significant results are in the higher risk groups. The education programme rather than cognitive skills, then, seems to follow more accurately the predictions of Andrews, Ross and colleagues.

The future

It is tempting to think that the apparently weak performance of the Cognitive Skills Programme in Canadian prisons over the past five years will lead to a renewed interest in education, as both a response to prisoner needs and as a contributor to offender rehabilitation. The positive results being generated by the research into the effectiveness of the former university programme in British Columbia and a revitalised (and privatised) basic and secondary programme in Ontario are hopeful signs. Given the public mood and the continued hysteria about crime displayed in the media, however – the context reviewed earlier – it is doubtful that the indirect, long-term and humanist claims made on behalf of prisoner education will be able to flourish. Instead, the cognitive psychologists having opened the door to a New Medical Model with their claim for a causal link between thinking and crime, may now have to watch as their colleagues in corrections turn for a magic solution to a new exclusive circle of clinicians, biologists and neurophysiologists.

The recent spate of books on the operation of the brain, what has been called a 'turning point . . . in the nature of human self-consciousness', promises to 'fix' the brain and thus be able to 'correct' thinking chemically or intrusively. Thus, 'What was hidden before is hidden no longer', thanks to new advances in brain scanning technology. For young people, we will soon be able to ' . . . identify and ameliorate subclinical sociopathologies earlier and more effectively . . .' and in terms of the law 'Such insight will . . . permit better informed application of our existing rules concerning responsibility, sentencing, and corrective incarceration . . .' (Churchland, 1995: 16). Stuart Yudofsky of the Baylor College of Medicine claims that with the expected advances in brain physiology ' . . . we're going to be able to diagnose many people who are biologically brain-prone to violence . . . we must trade our traditional concept

of justice based on guilt and punishment for a medical model based on prevention, diagnosis and treatment.' C. Ray Jeffrey at Florida State University has
gone so far as to demand that science ' . . . must tell us what individuals will or
will not become criminals, what individuals will or will not become victims,
and what law enforcement strategies will or will not work' (Gibbs, 1995: 102).
In Canada, Robert Hare at the University of British Columbia has developed a
psychopathy checklist that claims to identify psychopaths – individuals without
conscience – and argues that the only practical treatment is surgical or chemical,
not therapeutic or cognitive (Hare, 1993). Other researchers are making
dramatic claims about the link between low levels of the neurotransmitter
Sorotonin and aggression, particularly with impulsive behaviour in young males
(Lynn-Brown, 1994; Wright, 1995).

We have been down a road like this before, starting with phrenology and
criminal atavism and continuing with the eugenics bad gene theories and mental
deficiency in the 1920s, hormonal imbalance in the 1930s, the twin studies of
the 1940s, neurological disorders (EEGs) and mesomorphs in the 1950s, XYY
genes and Episodic Dyscontrol Syndrome in the 1960s, and Testosterone theories
in the 1970s. Despite the assurances of scientists in these decades, there appears
to have been ' . . . little empirical justification for the remarkable historical
resiliency of the biomedical approach to crime' (Nassi and Abramowitz, 1976).

We stand now poised before a new century, a new millennium, filled with
irrational fears about the endemic behaviours of our fellows, listening to the
siren song of science predicting a safe society through chemistry, and yet we
remain fundamentally humane enough to know better. Unwilling to face up to
the personal, cultural and economic costs of the sociological explanation that
most crime may in fact be the ' . . . not very surprising reaction of normal
people to oppressive circumstances' (Wright, 1995: 71), we are also constitution-
ally uneasy about the ethics of incapacitation through extended incarceration,
as well as chemical or surgical intrusions into the mind and soul of the
individual. This context of indecision has opened the door to a merry-go-
round of correctional policies, none of which have done more than advance
careers, enhance professionalism and cost money – to say nothing of the human
costs to those who were forced to experience the various intrusive treatments.

Throughout all this period educators have been teaching prisoners to read
and write, to calculate, create, build, think and value. While no cure-all for the
individual quirks or social forces that lead some people to commit crimes, it
has proven to be decisive for some, beneficial to all and as social policy a credit
to the nation that sponsors it. One can only hope that educators in Canada and
elsewhere will continue to assert its value, demonstrate its effectiveness and
work to persuade the public that a context of fear and hate will only produce
more of the same. As one prisoner put it so eloquently and simply, ' . . . you
create Spartan conditions, you're gonna get gladiators' (Worth, 1995: 44).

References

Andrews, D (1986) 'The risk principle of case classification: An outcome evaluation with young adult probationers', *Canadian Journal of Criminology*, v 28:4, pp 377–84.

Andrews, D (1990) 'Does correctional treatment work? A clinically relevant and psychologically informed meta-analysis', *Criminology*, v 28:3, pp 369–404.

Benson, I (1993) 'Report on Cog Skills Visit', correspondence, November

Churchland, P (1995) 'Our three pound engine', *Times Higher Education Supplement*, 14 April, p 16.

Cormier, R (1994) 'Reducing re-offending: The steps Canada is taking', *Prison Service Journal*, No 93, pp 47–50.

Cressey, D R (1960) 'Limitations on organizational treatment in the modern prison', in Cloward, R, *et al* (eds) *Theoretical Studies in Social Organization of the Prison*, Social Science Research Council.

Duguid, S (1987) 'Democratic praxis and prison education', *The Howard Journal of Criminal Justice*, v 26:1, pp 57–65.

Duguid, S (1996) 'Prison education and rehabilitation', *Journal of Correctional Education*, in press

Fox, F (1976) Speech in Vancouver, Vancouver *Sun*, 30 October.

Furtado, A and Johnson, D (1980) 'Education and rehabilitation in a prison setting', *Journal of Offender Counseling, Services, Rehabilitation*, v 4:3, pp 247–73.

Gehring, T (1988) 'The connection between democracy and cognitive processes in correctional education', *Journal of Correctional Education*, v 39:2, pp 13, 62–70.

Gendreau, P and Ross, R (1987) 'Revivification of rehabilitation: Evidence from the 1980's', *Justice Quarterly*, v 4:3, pp 349–407.

Gibbs, W (1995) 'Seeking the criminal element', *Scientific American*, March, pp 100–107.

Graff, H (1979) *The Literacy Myth*, Academic Press.

Hare, T (1993) *Without Conscience: The Disturbing World of the Psychopaths Among Us*, Simon and Schuster.

Holden, C (1975) 'Prisons: Faith in rehabilitation is suffering a collapse', *Science*, v 188:4190, pp 815–817.

Irwin, J (1973) *An Evaluation of Newgate and other prison education programs*, Final Report, March.

Knights, W (1982) *The Scholarly Community within federal prisons in the Pacific Region*, University of Victoria Program staff document.

Lab, S and Whitehead, J (1990) 'From nothing works to the appropriate works: The latest stop on the search for the Holy Grail', *Criminology*, v 28:3.

LaBar, C, *et al* Practical reasoning in corrections education', *Canadian Journal of Education*, v 8:3, pp 263–273.

Lynn-Brown, S, *et al* (1994) 'Serotonin and aggression', *Journal of Offender Rehabilitation*, v 21:3x4.

MacKenzie, D *et al* (1995) 'Boot Camp prisons and recidivism in eight states', *Criminology*, v 33:3, pp 327–357.

Martinson, R (1974) 'What Works? Questions and Answers about Prison Reform', *Public Interest*, Spring, pp 22–54.

Morris, N (1974) *The Future of Imprisonment*, University of Chicago Press.

Motiuk, L, and Belcourt, R (1996) 'Profiling the Canadian federal sex offender population', *Forum on Corrections Research*, v 8:2, pp 3–7.

Mott, J (1985) 'Adult prisons and prisoners in England and Wales, 1970–1982: A review of the findings of research', Home Office Research Study No 84, HMSO.

Nassi, A and Abramowitz, S. (1976) 'From phrenology to psychosurgery and back again: Biological studies of criminology', *American Journal of Orthopsychiatry*, v 46:4, pp 591–607.

Nuffield, J (1982) *Parole Decision-Making in Canada: Research Towards Decision Guidelines*, Solicitor General of Canada, Communication Division.

Peretti, P (1969) 'Educational rehabilitation: Prisoner attitude and inmate attendance', *Prison Journal*, v 8:3, pp 40–45.

Pillsbury, A (1995) 'Why are we ignored? The peculiar place of experts in the current debate about crime and justice', *Criminal Law Bulletin*, v 31:4, pp 305–336.

Posner, R (1995) 'The most punitive nation', *Times Literary Supplement*, 1 September.

Robinson, D (1995) *The Impact of Cognitive Skills Training on Post-Release Recidivism among Canadian Federal Offenders*, Correctional Service of Canada Research Division.

Ross, R (1985) *Time To Think: A Cognitive Model of Delinquency Prevention and Offender Rehabilitation*, Institute for Social Sciences and Arts.

Ross, R, Fabiano, E and Ewles, C (1988) 'Reasoning and rehabilitation', *International Journal of Offender Therapy and Comparative Criminology*, v 32:1, pp 29–35.

Rothman D (1994) 'The crime of punishment', *New York Review of Books*, 17 February, pp 34–38.

Sawatsky, J (1985) *Review of Offender Support Programs*, Correctional Service of Canada (Pacific Region).

Stewart, L and Millson, W (1995) 'Offender motivation for treatment as a responsivity factor', *Forum of Corrections Research*, v 7:3. pp 5–7.

Trevelyan, D (1981) 'Education as part of the concept of positive custody', *Coombe Lodge Reports*, v. 14:2, pp. 81–84.

Trotter, S and Warren, J (1974) 'The carrot, the stick and the prisoner', *Science News*, v 105, pp 180–181.

Worth, R (1995) 'A model prison', *Atlantic Monthly*, November, pp 38–44.

Wright, R (1995) 'The biology of violence', *New Yorker*, 13 March, pp 68–77.

Notes

[1] Cited in Toronto *Globe and Mail*, 23 March 1996.

[2] Canada had 596 homicides in 1994 compared to 600 in 1974, the rate of homicides per 100,000 population decreasing from 2.62 to 2.04. Meanwhile, the number of Canadians per police officer increased over the same 20-year period to 523 from 467. Toronto *Globe and Mail*, 16 December 1995.

[3] Richard Posner says that the probability of apprehension in the US is 'poor', thereby lowering the expected cost of punishment and making crime a more 'reasonable' economic activity (Posner, 1995).

[4] The California Three Strikes Law mandates that persons with two prior convictions for a serious offence will receive 25 years to life in prison following a conviction of *any* subsequent felony. There are some 500 felonies in California Law that will support a Third Strike. Estimates in California are that the law will result in an additional 80,000 prisoners by 1999, 149,000 by 2004 and 274,000 by 2026 (Pillsbury 1995, p 312).

[5] There are currently 164 prisoners designated as Dangerous Offenders in Canada. Since 1977, four people with this label have been paroled and 10 have died in prison.

[6] A study of eight boot camp programmes in eight states found ' . . . no significant

reduction in recidivism for programme graduates . . . In one state, Georgia, Boot Camp releasees did worse than parolees' (MacKenzie, 1995, p 352).

[7] American attitudes are changing quickly. Many states now have Sexual Predator Laws which impose mandatory treatment, community registration upon release and detention for life if required.

[8] Cressey is quite blunt in his scepticism of this agenda, noting that prisoners remain unconvinced that the prison is being run to treat or help them and they ' . . . cooperate . . . not to get treatment, but to avoid institutional punishments and to secure a release from the punitive aspects of imprisonment as soon as possible' (Cressey, 1960, p 100).

[9] Norman Carlson, speech to Florida Council on Crime and Delinquency, reported in Vancouver *Sun*, 8 July 1976. Prison policy in the United Kingdom was going through the same process. In 1969, at the time of the publication of the White Paper *People in Prison*, the UK Prison Service ' . . . remained officially committed to the view, admittedly with some caveats, that the treatment and training provided in the prisons, or new and better forms suggested by research findings, could reform and rehabilitate offenders and thereby reduce the likelihood of their re-offending and reconviction'. In the White Paper this appeared as a mandate to encourage offenders to ' . . . lead a good and useful life'. By the time of the next official review, the 1977 *Prisons and the Prisoner*, the conclusion was that ' . . . research findings give little support to the view that imprisonment can directly alter the long term behaviour of prisoners'. The report urged the abandonment of concern with either the origins of crime or with post-release recidivism studies and instead to focus on 'management of prisons'. Several major studies in the UK in the late 1970s concluded that ' . . . no penal measure has been demonstrated to have more rehabilitative or deterrent effect than another' (Mott, 1985, pp 2–4).

[10] *MacLeans* magazine, 21 March 1977. In England the term used after the May Report (1979) was 'Positive Custody, the point being . . . if a man wants to reform himself, then it is up to us, within the resources available, to provide the means by which he can do so' (Trevelyan, 1981).

[11] While the issue of false positives and inconclusive scientific evidence continues to hold back the implementation of a fully medicalised criminology, the adherents of such an approach believe it is only a matter of time. Their argument gains strength from the obvious failure of the 'nothing works' approach and the evidence that a very small percentage of delinquents and criminals commit well over half of known criminal acts. Thus Jeffrey (Criminologist, Florida State) argued that ' . . . attention must focus on the 5 per cent of the delinquent population who commit 50 per cent of the offences . . . This effort must identify high-risk persons at an early age and place them in treatment programmes *before* they have committed the 10 to 20 major felonies characteristic of the career criminal' (Gibbs, 1995, p 107).

[12] This language clearly strikes a chord with the public. Following a particularly brutal killing of an elderly couple in Montreal the judge in passing sentence on one of the young men involved concluded that while the crimes are horrible, ' . . . it does not mean you are a horrible person. We want to find out what your *needs* are' (Vancouver *Sun*, 27 January 1996).

[13] Prediction systems almost always suffer from 'overprediction'. 'Assume that one person out of a hundred will kill: a low "base rate". Assume also that an exceptionally accurate test is created which differentiates with 95 per cent effectiveness those who will kill from those who will not. If 100,000 people were tested, out of the 100 who would kill, 95 would be isolated. Unfortunately, out of the 99,900 who would

not kill, 4,995 people would also be isolated as potential killers. In these circumstances, it is clear that we could not justify incarcerating all 5,090 people.' In fact most predictive devices can only achieve about 50 per cent accuracy (Nuffield, 1982, p 16).

[14] Tentative results from the first phase of the research were as follows:

SIR Category	Predicted Success Rate	Actual Success Rate
A (4 out of 5 will not re-offend)	80%	98%
B (2 out of 3 will not re-offend)	66%	86%
C (1 out of 2 will not re-offend)	50%	77%
D (2 out of 5 will not re-offend)	40%	66%
E (1 out of 3 will not re-offend)	33%	60%

[15] In examining in more detail a sub-group prisoner-students (n–103) who served all or most of their sentence in maximum security and would therefore logically fall into the higher risk category, the study found direct correlations between number of credits earned, number of semesters completed, grade point average and 'intensity of engagement' with success and 'beating' their SIR prediction. Thus 74 per cent, the 38 students with a grade point average of 'A' or 'B', were successful after release, dramatically outperforming their SIR predicted success rate of 51 per cent. The 47 students with a 'C' average had a predicted success rate after release of 47 per cent, and in this case 60 per cent were in fact successful. Only 50 per cent of the 18 students with a 'D' grade point average, on the other hand, were successful, a mere one per cent improvement on their SIR prediction.

Chapter Three

The foundations of prison education in the People's Republic of China

Guo Xiang and Xu Zhangrun, China University of Political Science and Law, Beijing

The contemporary definition of the prison education and training system in China comes from the *'prison reform movement'* (*yuzhi gailiang yundong*) undertaken at the beginning of the 20th century.[1] As the gateway of the *Qing* Empire to the West had been opened in the late imperial era, we have to realise that from the very beginning of contact with, and enquiry about, western institutions and concepts, the Chinese studied the Western prison system.

At that time, concerned by China's repeated defeats at the hands of the Western Powers and Japan, Chinese intellectuals endeavoured to trace the roots of China's weakness, and regarded Western countries as more advanced models which China should ape at every step without any questions. Hence we can understand why Chinese intellectuals paid attention to prison education and inmates' training whilst they were intending to reform and rejuvenate China comprehensively.[2]

Although Chinese tradition has long stressed the need for criminals to undergo a form of 'instruction' (*jiao hua*), this was generally considered as a form of political-moral preaching. Thus even though laws were publicly promulgated, they were invariably regarded as 'aiding instruction' and the system of punishment and its implementation were all, in reality, no more than a process of political instruction. Thus, even though the great sage Mencius had suggested that it was possible to re-train in his statement that the superior man could draw 'from the whole Kingdom the most talented of individuals and teach and nourish them' (*de tianxia yingcai er jiaoyuzhi*)[3] when this idea was applied to prison re-training schemes, it led to a situation whereby the old adage about never 'mistaking a sow's ear for a silk purse' (*zhe yatou bushi na yatou*) became appropriate.[4] Nevertheless, the meaning given to education at that time cannot be assumed to be identical to that which is in use today.

In this context, during the period of *Prison reform*, China's legal scholars began to draw lessons from Western law and utilised Western legal canons as the basis upon which to draft their own legislation. One of the results was *The Draft of Qing Dynasty Prison Law* (*Daqing JianyuLu Caoan*) within which a distinction was made between 'education' (*jiaoyue*) and 'instruction' (*jiaohui*). Henceforth, 'education' was associated with intellectual development and vocational training, while 'instruction' was identified with regimes of moral training. This distinction remained intact right up to the 1950s when, because of a series of significant yet unforeseen political changes in China, the legal meaning of a whole range of terms began to be modified. Nevertheless, even during periods such as this one where massive changes were taking place, one could suggest that all such changes were charted using political, moral and theoretical co-ordinates which were drawn from the traditions outlined above. Hence, in *The Regulations on Reform Through Labour of the People's Republic of China* (abbreviated as *Regulation* hereafter), which was promulgated in 1954 and was replaced by the *The Prison Law of The People's Republic of China* (abbreviated as *Prison Law* hereafter) in 1994, one finds the term 'Reform through Education' incorporating both the notions of 'education' and of 'instruction'. The significant starting point of the distinction between 'instruction' and 'education' was the enactment of the *Prison Law* which will be mentioned later.[5]

The purpose of this modest treatise is to offer an objective introduction to Chinese prison education and to reveal the relationship between the socio-historical beginnings and development of these institutions and special factors within Chinese culture. Also, in the terms of etymology and Confucian hermeneutics, this chapter explores briefly a few ironic terms or 'discourses' of the penal system in China and attempts to identify the differences and integrations of them, by comparing them with each other. Moreover, in doing so, it will examine their impacts on the existing institutions.

The main types of prison education

Basically, from the viewpoint of the order of things, this chapter will look closely at the five elements of education in China's prisons.

Law education

Law education is designed to ensure that prisoners know, understand and respect the law. Moreover, it aims to cultivate a respect for the rights and responsibilities of the citizen as outlined in the Constitution and to designate certain activities as appropriate for prisoners. The development of the contemporary legal system from the time of the *Qing* Dynasty onwards is demonstrated. It is shown that while this system has subsequently gone through a range of different stages and periods of modification, it has continued to exist right through until the most recent period, when the lessons of the past have once again emerged. Under the influence of the aforementioned political-moral and ethical tradition, ordinary people in China have long regarded the legal regulation of private and social action as at best alien and at worst downright intrusive. Thus, while Chinese are sometimes involved in litigation, the overwhelming consensus is that law is not a process whereby rights and responsibilities are balanced justly, but is, in essence, the 'Law of the King' (*wangfa*).[6] Thus, the system of law education over the last two decades has been at pains to lay out clearly what acts are regarded as criminal, what the differences are between criminals and victims and the relationship between crime and punishment. These matters are introduced on the basis of the rights and obligations of citizens under the processes of constitutionalism. Generally speaking, it is constitutional law, criminal law, criminal procedure law, prison law, and marriage law which are covered in law education programmes for prisoners within Chinese prisons. Due to the low level of education of many of the prisoners, however, instruction in the field of law education is often very limited, for the literacy levels of prisoners often mean that it is impossible for them to understand the Chinese characters used in the codes or regulations. Hence, when it comes to teaching content, educators can offer only a very basic understanding of the codes and then promote this understanding amongst the prisoners to allow them to develop a concept of legal systems. In establishing a legal system curriculum to enable people to understand legal processes in China, specialist professionals and teachers are employed to teach legal knowledge, or special guest lecturers from law-related areas are invited into the prisons. Sometimes, courts that are hearing cases with special educational significance for the criminals are convened and heard in prisons, to teach the prisoners some lessons about the law. China has already completed its first-ever major campaign to popularise legal knowledge (*pufa*) and is currently implementing its second five-year legal popularisation programme. While these programmes are designed to educate all members of society about the law, prisoners form a very clear sub-group within this programme.

Moral education

Moral education is an important component of the educational transformation process undertaken in China; it could even be said to be the most important and effective educational procedure undertaken in the reform of prisoners. Especially when combined with the moral practices of the correctional officers in the prisons, it can be said that this will prove to be decisive in the process of transforming the prisoners and from this is derived and developed an authentic Chinese punishment system. This can best be expressed by the term *ganhua*, which has no direct English equivalent, but which could nevertheless be rendered as 'helping people to change' or, even more appropriately, 'setting an example by which to transform people while helping them to change'. That is to say, the prisons, as well as the correctional officers who implement policy in the system, constitute the basic pillars upon which an ethical and emotive procedure is put into place. It is through this procedure that there is an emotional exchange undertaken and this all takes place under the traditional Confucian code of 'benevolence' or, more appropriately, Confucian humanitarianism or Confucian humanity (*ren*). It is the actualisation of this that leads to an emotive exchange with the inmates and this then comes to form the basic structure of *ren*. In turn, the changes in the inmates' emotions push along, influence and finally transform the basic methodology of the whole penal system. In the classical *Chinese Text of Character Explanations (Shuowen Jiezi)*, the term *gan* is said to mean the production of feeling that is powerful enough to move the heart, whereas the term *hua* is rendered as an action or actions on the part of a subject that brings forth change. Therefore, the term *ganhua* combines the emotional state of bringing forth change with the practical action of a person actually inducing it. Through *ganhua* authorities utilise the ethical and emotional ties they build up with their charges to bring forth a change in the individual as well as in their perspective of society. This idea, along with the traditional Chinese concept of 'culture' (*wenhua*) – which should be understood as being much broader than the equivalent notion in English usage – and transformation, all begin to tie into the idea of 'taming' or 'domesticating' (*xunhua*). Hence, things which at first seem to have no relation to one another are, in fact, tied together as part of the same process. Thus, while the system appears to be very 'legalistic' and, in the words of Confucius, 'People led by laws and uniform forms of implemented punishment',[7] it actually constitutes the basis upon which morality and uniformity can be obtained on the basis of laws of propriety.

Apart from these traditional concerns, however, one also needs to recognise the affinity these notions have with Western transformational practices. One can see here how the moral ordering implied by the traditional tactics of government and behaviour control begin to fan out as they are imported into this concept of *ganhua*. More realistically – and from the perspective of Chinese culture – this notion of *ganhua* transformation is a product of the Chinese concept of moral self-cultivation. That is to say, under the influence of the Confucian notion of *ren*, a practice is adopted whereby one learns to treat others as one would wish oneself to be treated. To summarise this process by using a very positive colloquial Chinese expression, it could be said to mean 'one good turn deserves another'. The '*Zhongshu*'[8] or the golden rule, is that: 'Wishing to establish his own character, he also establishes the characters of others, and wishing to be prominent himself, he also helps others to be prominent.'[9] It could also be expressed as 'Do not do to others what you would not want others to do to you'.[10] The golden rule is also negatively stated because of the emphasis on self-cultivation. As noted by Professor Tu Wei-ming, 'Underlying the golden rule, then, is the premise that conscientiousness (*zhong*) and altruism (*shu*) are not far from the way'.[11] The inner demand for being truthful to one's humane self is inseparable from the social need to care for others; and the learning for self-realisation is also the learning for harmonising human relations'.[12] Therefore, within traditional Chinese ethical philosophy, this expression could be said to stand for the basis upon which all forms of interpersonal relations are conducted. It can also be said to constitute the basis upon which all business is handled and, in so doing, it sets the standard for an honest and tolerant system to be established.

With this kind of thinking as a basis, Chinese people, when undergoing education, quite often try very hard to place themselves in the other person's shoes. On the other hand, it is the student's responsibility to 'simply turn round and seek the cause of his failure in himself'.[13] The educators also try to think of how their students must feel, and this form of 'displacement' constitutes one of the simplest yet most effective methods. This is because it easily allows for mutual acceptance. Thus, while this method of displacement may seem opaque, it is, in fact, the most economical of means. For example, in order to help prisoners reflect upon their crimes, teachers not only enlighten *via* the explanation of laws and reasoned argument, but also attempt to get offenders to acknowledge responsibility for their behaviour. As they begin to acknowledge responsibility, they also come to realise the harm they have caused their victims – all this takes place through the emotive exchange of *ren* – and they also begin to occupy the abject position. This, in turn, leads them to ask of themselves: 'what if I were the victim?' The result of such self-questioning is a process of self-shaming brought on by the self-educative role of this question. In reality, this all goes to show that a certain level of flexibility in the system is necessary if results are to be achieved. The most compelling evidence of the success of this approach comes from the practices adopted in the 1950s in China in relation to Japanese war criminals. The common cultural reference points of Japanese and Chinese people, and especially their common Confucian heritage, meant that the Chinese authorities were able to utilise these sorts of procedures in the re-education of Japanese war criminals with startling results.[14] So it is somehow true that, to a certain extent, as contended by John Braithwaite, 'reintegrative shaming' can resolve the crime problem from the corporate board to the streets, from one culture to the next.[15]

Second, the notion of *ganhua* is the product of a very particular way of thinking in traditional China which turns on notions of intuition, body and realisation. Zen Buddhist (*Chanzong*) writings on the relationship between body, soul and intuition form the most obvious reference point here. It was through this mode of thinking, rather than Western notions of reason, that Chinese people in traditional times came to an understanding of their world. Moreover, what was special about this particular form of thinking was that it appealed directly to a holistic sense of body and soul and, in so doing, crossed all the various levels of logical reasoning and offered a means by which one could get a sense of how others felt. This so-called ability to get to the essence of all things or to the inner realm of soul (*zhizhi benxin*), is critical to an understanding of the differences between the logics of the East and those of the West. When this form of logic is used in the Chinese prison educational system, it effectively makes the criminal emotively connect with, and learn from, the simple morality offered to them by the correctional officer. In this way the criminal unconsciously take these feelings on board and, on the basis of this discrete process, begin to modify behaviour and to recognise that crime does not pay.

In recent decades, China has undergone substantial change and the role of, as well as the lessons learnt from the past about, *ganhua* appears no longer quite as self-evident as was the case previously. This may well have significant implications for China's future prison strategies, and we will address this issue a little later in the chapter.

As an apparent digression, it would be instructive to compare the *ganhua* with a few other terms in the Chinese penal system. The word for imprisonment in traditional Chinese is *tu*. In contemporary Chinese, the Character *tu* combines with *Xing* and forms the word *tuxing*, which can be translated as 'a loss of freedom' in the modern penological understanding. In ancient Chinese, the character *tu* was often substituted for the character *nu* which had a very similar pronunciation but a different meaning. The character *nu* meant 'to engage in physical labour'. Hence, the compound *tuxing* when read as *nuxing*, translated literally as forced labour undertaken through penal servitude, an association which persists in modern popular Chinese. This popular traditional association between forced labour and penal servitude was further reinforced by similar associations made in the popular rhyming dictionary of traditional times, the *Ji Yun*. In this text, *tu* was explained as corresponding with the character *nu* which meant enslavement. Such was the power of this form of coupling that it even found its way into the classical legal codes. In the highly authoritative *Tang Dynasty code and its explanation (Tanglu Shuyi)*, the character *tu* was described as having the character and meaning of *nu*.[16] Through this association with *nu*, the text asserts, the full implications of imprisonment become apparent: keeping criminals in conditions of enslavement and disgrace. Because China is a country where the past is revered, these connotations were not confined to the *Tang* Dynasty but were read into the legal codes of all subsequent dynasties. In this way, these values became part of the legal assumptions of each subsequent regime and part of the assumed culture co-ordinates of the entire nation. They became part of the knowledge that, in another context, Paul Veyne once described as the large zone of the unexpressed which guides action but that is so deeply assumed it is never articulated or even consciously thought.[17] Penal labour as punishment therefore became an unconscious yet widely accepted notion long after the linguistic association between *tu* and *nu* died away. Moreover, it had become such an ingrained association that it was scarred on to the national mind-set and no subsequent reformist agenda was able fully to erase it.

The history of post-1949 penal discourse stands as a testimony to this struggle for erasure. It is a history of a struggle over this word (*tu*) yet the vapour trails of the past, despite the very best of Marxist intent, have never cleared enough to allow the transformationist agenda to be free of its ugly twin. The history of 'reform through labour' reads like a constant battle between these two meanings. From the early accounts of prisons needing to produce to survive, through to more recent cases of labour being exploited for personal gain, the history of penal institutions in contemporary China reads like a 'two line struggle' over this single word and its deeper meaning.[18]

If we trace further back, we can find that there is a long tradition in China that separates mental and manual labour and this was largely predicated upon class differences. This difference is well summed up in the Confucian saying that 'those who work with their heads rule while those who work with their hands are ruled'. Liang Shu-ming, called 'the Last Confucian' by Dr Alitto,[19] has insisted that while traditional Confucian philosophy had made this distinction, it had placed no moral value on it. It was, he implied, simply the way things were, or the fact of the division of labour in society.[20] Indeed, Liang goes on to suggest, in a manner similar to contemporary Chinese readings of Marx, that Confucius held labouring people in high esteem and that people should be solicitous of them and recognise them as the creators of all wealth. While this may well be true, it was an argument that did little to decouple the long-held association between physical labour and punishment. Physical labour, in the penal system in China, as in that of the West before the latter half of this century,[21] has traditionally been regarded as a form of enslavement and disgrace. This perspective is graphically illustrated in the penal vocabulary that had operated in traditional times and which, interestingly enough, is still in use today as mentioned above. Hence, it would not be a concern but for the fact that such past meanings are all too often still active in the unconscious implications of words in modern usage. The etymology of Chinese words like 'ganhua' and 'tu', 'nu' are a striking testimony to this argument.

General knowledge course (literacy and numeracy education)

In the last decade, there has been a significant increase in the amount of time and space devoted to vocational, general knowledge and technical training. This has now reached the stage where such forms of education are undertaken throughout the country. To give some concrete examples here, practically every prison has established itself as a 'special educational institution'. This trend has taken hold particularly in those prisons near cities or in suburbs and which are engaged in industrial production. All these institutions have been involved in education and training programmes designed to eliminate illiteracy and raise the level of prisoners' skills. The Bureau of Prison Administration under the central leadership of the Ministry of Justice and each province and municipality under central control, as well as those of the autonomous regions, have all established professional departments to carry out this work and manage these programmes. To protect the quality of teaching and check on content, regular checks are made and comparisons carried out. In addition, exhibitions and competitions are also conducted to try to promote innovation and excellence.

In the Chinese Ministry of Justice documents on 'special educational institutions' (which are established by the prisons), there are regulations which stipulate that any prison that wants to establish itself as a 'special educational institution' must learn 'three lessons' before it becomes eligible. The three lessons call for an overall teaching management structure to be established, qualified teachers to be hired and classroom space to be allocated, equipment arranged for and teaching methodologies developed. When these criteria have been met, standardised and systematised, then the authorities, to be eligible for the title of being a 'special educational institution', must ensure that between 70 per cent and 90 per cent of all eligible prisoners are offered education. In terms of the facilities and activities conducted in these 'special educational institutions', it can be said that a teaching system must be instituted, class space created, teaching classes organised, the quality of teaching personnel guaranteed, both the teaching curriculum and administration of teaching systematised, lecturing rooms arranged, teaching times regularised and teaching requirements standardised. On the basis of the draft regulations entitled *The Detailed Regulations on Higher Levels of Inspection, Checking and then Accepting the 'Special Educational Institutions'*, formulated by the Ministry of Justice in December 1990, all special institutions at the provincial level must reach the following standards, which are then tested by two examinations: the 'four negations' and the 'ten ordinaries'. To pass the four negations necessitates:

1)   that there are no instances of anything such as murder, arson, violence or chaos in the prison which disrupt its orderly functioning;
2)   that the transformation rate for hardened or serious offenders within the institution needs to be over 40 per cent;
3)   that the pass rate of prisoners in political courses be over 90 per cent; and,
4)   that within the prison itself, the annual rate of crime does not exceed 0.15 per cent in the case of industrial prison work units and 0.2 per cent in the case of prison farms.

The ten ordinary examinations work off a standard checklist relating to rates of escape, rates of abnormal deaths, and the rates at which the 'three lessons' have been learnt. It also checks on the class periods, teaching performances and equipment used, as well as any breaches of discipline on the part of correctional officers, and the completion of production quotas. Institutions are tested once every two years and those that cannot maintain their standards are demoted by degree or stripped of their title and have all bonuses cancelled. Any institution which is able to fulfill the above criteria and then raise its standard can, after checking by the Ministry of Justice's committee for the checking and approval of higher education special education institutions, be awarded 'model status'. Currently, there are only a very small number of these model institutions, but it is also true to say that standards within all institutions are rising rapidly, particularly in the prisons located close to cities.

To regularise the implementation of educational transformation, the Ministry of Justice, the State Education Commission and the Ministry of Personnel have together promulgated the *Directive Concerning the Strengthening of Technical and Cultural Education Personnel in the Reform Through Labour and Reform Through Education Institutions 1986.* This directive includes some concrete demands regarding the position of educators, the role of prisoners in learning literacy, numeracy and skills, and the types of checks that would be carried out and awards made. In terms of concrete organisational matters, educational departments were established by the bureau of prison administration in each province, by municipalities directly under the Central Government, and by autonomous regions. The most important role of such departments was to carry out macro-level planning of teaching and relate, co-ordinate and resolve problems associated with teaching in a prison setting. The education sections of the prison would, on the basis of the specific characteristics of the production activity carried out by the prison, institute concrete organisational forms to facilitate study. This would be led by an office of training and research. The task of the office of training and research is to arrange tuition times, teaching staff, put into effect tests and examinations and do anything else deemed necessary to fulfill the requirements of the directive. From the above-mentioned directive, it is quite clear that orders always come from the top and filter down and, in many respects, this is a microcosm of how the whole Chinese political structure works. In the field also, we find a hierarchical order with interspersed branches leading outwards.

Ordinarily, prisoners work an eight-hour day and study about 10 hours per week, of which four hours are devoted to politics and three to culture and other forms of education respectively. Agricultural units of prison settings are allowed to vary this routine to take into account the seasonal nature of their production process, but they too must establish an annual teaching routine that is not less than 10 hours per week. Due to the relatively under-developed nature of such units, however, many of them fail to live up to expectations and therefore are in breach of the law. This is a situation that correctional institutions in just about all countries face at one time or another. In a country like China, which is still working on developing its legal structure, such a situation would seem to be unavoidable.

Technical and vocational training

Concerning the technical or professional training regime, the basic policy of Chinese prisons over recent years has been 'to establish reform, keep an eye on employment and serve the community'. What this all adds up to is the introduction of a number of technical training programmes that take into account the production activities for the correction of inmates and which also benefit and encourage the inmates to reform. This type of training is designed to fit with community needs and to increase the prospects of work for ex-prisoners. There are a number of ways in which technical training has been instituted in China's prison system and the four most important of these are discussed below.

First, short-term specialist courses. Inmates join classes which explain the uses of equipment, train them in its operation and teach them how to undertake simple maintenance. They do this alongside more general training programmes which explain such things as the rules governing the production process. This then enables inmates to undertake productive duties within the prison on the one hand, and to be technically competent to operate machinery on the other. So as to further enhance their skills base and thereby increase their employment opportunities upon release, intensive programmes are adopted in the immediate period prior to release which offer training in areas which can be taught very quickly, yet which still require some technical competence. For example, inmates are taught to use and maintain certain types of equipment, they are taught tailoring, hairdressing, cooking, carpentry, tiling, furniture making and restoration, electrical skills and basic horticulture.

Second, technical exemplification. This is designed to combine the needs of the classroom with practical experience. When prisoners are in vehicles or in the field, they are exposed to training on specific types of equipment which enable them to become familiar with their operation. This then allows them to operate such equipment and to know how it functions and what it is capable of doing.

Third, part-study, part-work. Allowing prisoners to undertake labour duties and, in so doing, allowing them some capacity for on-the-job training. This allows them to undergo a fairly simple form of job training.

Fourth, practice and traineeships. If conditions within prisons are conducive to the practice, then test sites or workshops should be established. This will allow the prisoners opportunities to practise their newly-developed skills, test those skills and improve their performance, as well as grasp certain technical details.

These various forms of technical and vocational training are provided to encourage prisoners and to increase their willingness to learn trades. In the Chinese prison system, there are a number of different levels of examination designed to test and grade inmates' technical skills. Generally, such testing is conducted by the local prison or prison administrative personnel department, and is conducted on the basis of the regulations outlined in *The Temporary Ordinances on Testing the Professional Competence of Labour*. In accordance with these regulations, each industrial department promulgates a calibrated set of standards for technical work in their own areas and, on the basis of this, strict tests are undertaken to ascertain the inmates' level of competence. On the basis of the standard achieved in any particular test, the prison personnel department is authorised to issue professional grade certificates which can then be used by the inmates, upon release, as an accreditation certificate when seeking employment.

Political education

The most important factors to be noted in this regard are general political education, an education on one's outlook on life, society and others, and an education about current political, economic and social conditions and future prospects. After 1949, it is true that in China 'Politics not only dominated life,' as commented by Julia Ching, 'it was life. Politics absorbed history, literature, economics and philosophy'.[22] Ironically, recent years have witnessed the ineffectual nature and the gradual fading out of the gospel of political education in the penal system. It could result from the low regard for political propaganda held by Chinese people in general, and by prisoners in particular, from the 1980s onwards. But it also reflects the socio-political concerns of the drafters. They were happy to leave the political colour of law vague and ambiguous because they feared that all attempts to stress politics would land them in 'innumerable difficulties'. And they were bored by the political concern of law-making.[23] The positive effects of this attitude towards the new *Prison Law* (1994) will be addressed in the next section.

The reforms of prison education in the prison law (1994)

Generally, in comparison with the *Regulation of Reform through Labour of The People's Republic of China*, it is clear that the articles and the arrangement and structure of the section regulating education or 'Reform through Education' in the *Prison Law of The People's Republic of China*, (1994) are far better organised. This could indicate attitudinal changes amongst Chinese legislators in both values and technique and also fundamental transformation in the process of Chinese politics and society.

First of all, the *Regulation* provided only a sketchy outline of requirements for education in Chapter Three, 'Reform through Labour and Reform through Education'. On the contrary, two Chapters, Five and Six, consisting of 17 Articles, are specific on the role of education in the *Prison Law*. Moreover, the 'Reform through Labour' has also been incorporated within the framework of education or the 'Reform through Education'. Literally, the concept of Reform through Labour no longer exists in the context of the code. Accordingly, in 1995 the Bureau of Reform through Labour under the leadership of the Ministry of Justice was also re-titled the Bureau of Prison Administration. To sum up, the so-called '*Reform through Labour*' with '*Chinese socialist characteristics*' which had been long-standing, ceased to exist and the legitimacy of *Reform through Labour* as a total prison system came to an end. This implies that the legislators developed penological thinking by emphasising the function of education rather than 'Labour' for the purpose of rehabilitation. That means, to a certain extent, the penal focus has shifted from slaving criminals' 'sinews and bones with toil'[24] (*Lao qi jinggu*) to 'cultivating their minds with rites and humanities' (*yang qi xinzhi*). In this regard, there was a dramatic change during the drafting of the prison law. Curiously, until October and November 1994, little more than one month before the *Prison Law* was enacted by the Standing Committee of National People's Congress, 'Reform through Labour' was still the title of the chapter and was separate from the chapter called 'reform through education' in the draft of the law. By a directive 'from above', the former was banished from the final formal context of the code which was enacted on 29 December 1994. There remain only two Articles, 69 and 70, in Chapter Five entitled 'The Reform through Education of Criminals'. Article 69 prescribes that 'all inmates who have abilities to work must take part in labour'; Article 70 states that 'According to inmates' individual circumstance, prisons organise them to work so as to correct their pernicious habits, cultivate the work habit, let them learn work skills and make preparation for employment after release.' By comparison, apart from all 11 Articles of two Chapters, out of 77 Articles of the *Regulation* the only other Articles relating to the *Reform through Labour* are 1, 18, 22, 52 and 72, Clause 3 in both Articles 68 and 69, Clause 4 of Article 71. Furthermore, words such as 'coercive labour' in the *Regulation* are also replaced by the words, in the *Prison Law*, such as 'must' (bixu) or 'should' which are neutral and moderate in Chinese. Hence 'labour' has become one of the means of 'education' in the logic of the *Prison Law*. The other significant fact is that the sense of 'Reform through Labour System with Chinese socialist characteristics' involving a belief in the superiority of so-called 'Marxism-Leninism-Maoism Labour theory', and the desire to perpetuate that theory in China's penal practice, melted away in public consciousness.

On the other hand 'labour' is still seen as prisoners' main daily occupation and is in some prisons located in remote and economically backward parts of China, possibly the *only* 'programme'. Again, it suggests that the Chinese way towards the construction of a legal system and the rule of law was, and still is, perplexed by the disjunction between prescription in law and reality in practice. There are earlier examples of this disjunction; when the *draft of Qing dynasty of Prison Law* prescribed 'religious instruction' to inmates as one of the requirements of prison institutions, it certainly could not achieve the desired results because the same religious background did not exist throughout China.[25] In the past century, modernisation was understood as an accelerating trend towards 'Westernisation' or more recently 'Americanisation'. It is difficult for the East to transplant Western values, concepts and institutions into their own, very different cultures. China is no exception.

Second, the *Regulation* classified prison education into four main sorts (Article 26): education about recognising guilt and keeping the law; education about current political affairs; education about labour and production; and general knowledge courses. Obviously, the value focus here was placed on recognising guilt and keeping the law in a framework of 'law education'; the 'general knowledge course' was the least important. This classification was typical of the times when political ideological 'grand claims' dominated all aspects of life and inmates were regarded as 'ghosts and monsters' in 1950s China. In comparison, what the *Prison Law* now prescribes is ideological education, general knowledge courses and technical (vocational) training. Ideological education includes 'education about law, morality, the current social-political-economic situation and policy, and future prospects of release'. It is noteworthy that the *Prison Law* includes moral, legal and other elements in the same context of 'ideological education'. Its positive side is to give 'law education' priority over the others, in particular, to 'moral education'. Further, the recognition of guilt and keeping the law were replaced by 'law education' with broader course contents than before. On the negative side, legislators still did not make a clear distinction between legal and political claims so that law education was almost absorbed by the ideological emphasis.

Last but not least, the new *Prison Law* highlights education for juvenile delinquents. The proportion of youth and juveniles in China's prisons has increased significantly from the 1980s onwards. They make up the main part of the prison population. The *Prison Law* includes a specific chapter governing education for juveniles and prescribes that priority should be given to 'general knowledge courses and technical (vocational) training'. However, even though they are normally involved in half a day's work and half a day's learning in normal penal practice, it is still regrettable that there are no strict provisions about the allocation of time on work and learning each day respectively. For the sake of safeguarding minors, there is room for improvement in the future.

Conclusion

In this chapter, we have been concerned with a general introduction to prison education and some of the ironies emerging from the etymology of the penal system of China. We find that there have been some real changes in this area in China, while there is still force in the old habits of thought which carries the meaning of the original words into new expressions. This would not be a concern but for the fact that such past meanings are all too often still active in unconsciously framing words into contemporary situations. We might hear a remote echo from the one end of the historical tube, but we cannot get a clear reading of it. As a result, the conflicts between value orientation of the 'new' and the 'old', ideological gospels and social reality are inevitable. *Ganhua*, for instance, the long-term programme which has been successful in the past, is in need of modification, since the moral order and social climate which enabled its success have now changed. This need for change has been precipitated by the changes in attitudes of the younger generation, not only of inmates, but also those of correctional officials. They believe that the proof of the pudding lies in the eating rather than in pursuing pies in the sky. Thus the interaction between man and the infrastructure will create a new space which recognises individualism and nurtures respect for human beings, rather than seeing power as a universal model by ignoring individualism and diminishing human dignity. In fact, all changes in China from the 1980s can been understood as one of the tendencies towards the emergence of what Max Weber calls 'rationalisation' in political, economic, educational and penal institutions.

As pointed out by Professor Stanley Cohen: 'In those parts of the world racked by state terror, drugs, wars and ethnic, nationalist or religious conflict, political violence certainly creates far more victims than regular criminal violence.'[26] We would like to add that this applies equally to a violent and dicatorial penal system.

Notes

[1] For a systematic critique on the process and the dilemma of *The Prison Reform Movement* in the late imperial era, see Xue Mei-qing (editor in chief), *The History of the Chinese Prison System,* Chap11, Mass Press, 1986, Beijing; Sheng Jia-ben's Narrative and Practice in Prison Reform, in *the Conference Proceedings of the International Forum on Chinese Legal History,* Shanxi People's Press, 1990, Xian; also Li Gui-lian, *Sheng Jia-ben and the Modernisation of the Chinese Legal system,* pp 134–44, Guangming Daily Press, 1989, Beijing.

[2] For the systematic exploration of Chinese intellectual cultural iconoclasm see Lin Yu-sheng, *The Crisis of Chinese Consciousness,* University of Wisconsin Press, 1979, Madison; also 'Radical Iconoclasm in the May Fourth Period and the Future of Chinese Liberalism', in Benjamin I Schwartz (ed), *Reflections on the May Fourth Movement,* Harvard University Press 1972. For another stimulating analysis of this topic in the light of Confucian symbolism see Tu Wei-ming, Confucianism: Symbol and Substance in Recent Times, in *Humanity and Self-Cultivation: Essays in Confucian Thought,* p 227 onwards, Asian Humanities Press, 1979, Berkeley, USA.

[3] *Mencius: Jinxin* (part 1).

[4] *Dream of the Red Mansion (Hong Lou Meng)*

[5] It is our contention that any attempts to come to grips with events in contemporary China require a through historical understanding of the Chinese penal system and we would argue that it is impossible to offer a clear explanation of the practices adopted in the Chinese so-called 'reform through labour' system without some understanding of this traditional notion of 'instruction' and the process of '*Prison Reform*'. In this way, contemporary Chinese institutions with an interest in prison education cannot be divorced from either traditional Confucian teachings or the gospel of Western ideals, liberalism or communism, in the past and at present. For details of Chinese studies on the Western prison system and concepts during the period of '*Prison Reform*', see Xu Zhangrun, 'From East to West: Inquiries on Western Prison System in the Late *Qing* Dynasty', in *Law Review of Nanjing University,* pp 38–49, Vol 2, No 2, 1995, Nanjing.

[6] For further details see Xu Zhangrun, *Penology,* China University of Political Science and Law Press, pp 226–30, 1991, Beijing.

[7] The whole sentence in *Analects* is: The Master said, 'If they be led by laws, and uniformity sought to be given them by punishment, they will try to avoid the punishment, but have no sense of shame. If they led by virtue, and uniformity sought to be given them by rules of propriety, they will have the sense of shame, and moreover will become good.' See *Analects,* 2: 23.

[8] Apart from the analysis given by Tu Wei-ming mentioned later, the interpretations about the concept of '*zhongshu*' in Confucius' thought given by Prof Qu Wan-li are also very accurate. For details, see *Selected Works of Qu Wan-li*, Vol 1, pp 303–12, Lianjing Publishing Co Ltd, 1985, Taibei.

[9] *Analects*, 6.28.

[10] *Analects*, 15.23; see also *The Doctrine of the Mean (Zhong-yong)*, 13.3.

[11] *The Doctrine Of the Mean (Zhong-yong)*, 13.3.

[12] For details see Tu Wei-ming, The Confucian Perception of Adulthood, in *Humanity and Self-Cultivation: Essays in Confucian Thought*, p 48, Asian Humanities Press, Berkeley, USA, 1979.

[13] *Mencius: Gongsun Chou* (part 1).

[14] For further details see Xu Zhangrun, On the Psychology of Japanese War Criminals, *Journal of China University of Political Science and Law*, Vol 4, 1989, Beijing.

[15] John Braithwaite, *Crime, Shame and Reintegration,* p 15, Cambridge University Press, 1989, Cambridge, UK.

[16] *Tang Code: Ming Li.*

[17] Paul Veyne, The Inventory of Difference, in *Economy and Society*, Vol 11, No 2, p 191, May 1982, London, UK.

[18] Re Michael Dutton and Xu Zhangrun forthcoming paper *Facing Difference: Relations, Changes and the Prison Sector in Contemporary China*.

[19] For details of Liang Shu-ming's life and thought, see Dr. Guy S. Alitto, *The Last Confucian: Liang Shu-ming and the Chinese Dilemma of Modernization*, University of California Press, 2nd ed. 1986, Berkeley, USA; Ma Dong-yu, *Biography of Liang Shu-ming*, Shanghai People's Press, 1991, Shanghai.

[20] Liang Shu-ming, *An outline of Chinese Arts*, pp 99–103, Bashu Press, Chengdu, 1986; also see Cai Shang-si, *A General Critique on Chinese Traditional Thoughts*, pp 29–31, Hunan People's Press, 1987, Changsha.

[21] For further details about the practice of punishment in the West, see *The Oxford History of Prison – the Practice of Punishment in Western Society*, Chapters 5–8, edited by Norval Morris and David J Rothman, Oxford University Press, Oxford, 1995, UK.

[22] Julia Ching, 'Probing China's soul' in F J Adelmann (ed), *Contemporary Chinese Philosophy*, p 83 Martinus Nijhoff Publishers, The Hague, Boston, 1982, USA.

[23] Interview with one of the drafters, 24 September 1994, Beijing.

[24] *Mencius: Gao zi* (part 2).

[25] Re Sidney D Gamble and John S Buegess, *Peking: A Social Survey,* p 311, Oxford University Press, 1921, UK.

[26] Stanley Cohen, Crime and Politics: Spot the difference, in *The British Journal of Sociology*, Vol 11, No 1, pp 1–21, May 1996, London.

Chapter Four

The prison service and education in England and Wales

W Forster, Department of Adult Education, University of Leicester

Robert Peel's Parliamentary Gaol Act of 1823 required the first significant provision of education in English prisons, calling for instruction in reading and writing in all prisons and requiring all authorities to appoint schoolmasters. Since that date, with different strengths and emphases at different times, education has regularly played a part in prison life.

This history, though, has been patchy. The nineteenth century saw a gradual erosion of much of the humanitarian spirit of Peel's Act, which had emerged partly from the broad reforming instincts of the late eighteenth and early nineteenth centuries. Whilst in the middle years of the nineteenth century much more repressive regimes developed, local autonomy managed to keep some flames alight and, indeed, the work of individual reformers such as Elizabeth Fry led to significant development in some locations.

The Prison Act of 1877 established our prison system very much as it is today and had the immediate effect of centralising the system. Whilst the consequent rules and regulations made provision for education, this was surrounded by proscription and rules rather than fuelled by imagination or humanitarian zeal.

It was not until the period after the First World War that significant developments were to be seen. This was the age of the voluntary teacher – there being no public resource available to pay for a cohort of professional staff – with some of these volunteers emerging from the prison service – Chaplains, Borstal housemasters – and others from outside the walls. Whilst many grim rules persisted, there was developing a view, partly amongst the public at large and partly from individuals such as Alexander Paterson within the Prison Service, that prison should be something more than retributive and unpleasant confinement and work. The evidence is that this voluntary activity – maybe because it was voluntary and pragmatic – gave rise to a much wider range of activity (debates, concerts, craft activities, for example) than hitherto. The impulse of the Second World War gave rise to an element of industrial training (in Maidstone and Wakefield Prisons) with a view to discharging prisoners into productive factory work.

So when, at the end of the war, the Prison Commission began to plan for an education service of its own, it did have to hand practical experience of what could be done within the prison walls.

The spirit of the post-war years, 'building a new world', was carried forward by the chairman of the then Prison Commission. He adhered to the 'better men and women' principle, articulated 50 years before in the Gladstone Report, and worked for a significant contribution from a professional education service, fully integrated into the penal system. To this end, he work with the Education Act of 1944 and planned a structure in collaboration with the Department of Education and Employment; the local authorities; and the Central Council for Physical Recreation; as well as calling upon the experience of the Army Bureau of Current Affairs. Ultimately – despite an awareness of the desperate shortage of resources and an intitial unwillingness on the part of some Local Education Authorities (LEAs) – a system was put in place which enabled LEAs to employ a cohort of educationalists to work in prisons in their region, reclaiming the cost of this exercise from the central government (ie, from the Home Office).

This set the overall pattern for the system that was in place until early in 1993. But it was not achieved immediately or easily. By 1958, there were still only 29 full-time education officers; the rest were part-time. Moreover, as well as the practical difficulties arising from this situation, there were (and still are) considerable cultural challenges to be met. Whilst the number of education staff in prison has now improved, the system keeps on having to cope both with one set of problems – pressure upon accommodation, industrial unrest within the Prison Service, riot and disorder – and with sudden swings in public opinion.

During 1992, the decision was taken to contract out the provision of educational services in prisons in England and Wales on a competitive tendering basis. In part, this policy reflected a general tendency in most public service areas by which the governmental agency 'bought in' the required services rather than supplied directly; but it was given impetus by the changing status of the Further Education (FE) Colleges and their relationship with the LEA. The FE Act removed the FE sector from LEA control with the effect that Home Office/LEA understanding and agreements could no longer be seen as committing colleges to provide a service in prisons.

National advertisements placed in August 1992 attracted 547 enquiries; 248 of these enquiries completed an initial questionnaire and, by October, 190 organisations were invited to tender for a wide variety of groupings of prisons. The number of organisations who actually tendered was 155 and, by early 1994, there were 45 suppliers to 125 prisons.

Of these suppliers, 39 are Colleges, one is a University, three are private training organisations, and two are LEA adult education services.

Inevitably, this process had led to a degree of disruption; education officers in particular saw their standing within the prison as potentially diminished (and were highly resistant to changes in condition of service), and many saw the line management responsibilities – employers, Home Office Prison Department, governor – as confused and confusing, as well as being concerned, in some cases, at being cut off from public services. The prison department saw itself as having a firmer grasp, via the contract, upon many aspects of the quality of service and a greater control of such areas as curriculum development and level of provision as well as finance.

It will be some time before many of the issues involved – professional and legal – will be resolved. But the period of flux gives the opportunity to review some of the fundamental issues of education in prisons.

Many education officers will detect little change in their day-to-day working lives: the contract will have gone to the original providing college or to a similar college. Others are finding significant changes and it is impossible to generalise about the pre-1993 situation, whereby the Home Office made payments to LEAs which in turn, 'employed' Prison Education Staff, usually via a local college. In some cases, the relationship with the college was remote and formal, in others the Education Officer was fully integrated into the institution; in one case at least, the college regarded the prison as an extension of itself and all staff could be required to teach there.

Current resource restrictions are bringing some areas of this relatively new contractual arrangement into question. As governors have fewer and fewer resources to allocate, so does the allocation to education reduce. And there are distinct signs that some colleges now regard the level of educational activity in their contracted prisons as being too small to be worth handling. The outcome of this – and one can only conjecture – could be that more and more contracts come into the hands of fewer and fewer providers, with all the problems which could emerge from the increasing remoteness of college management from the point of delivery and local issues and problems.

Recent years have thus been years of turmoil for the prison education officer, raising anxieties not only about the programme but about her/his own career and conditions of employment, but also about her/his positioning within the management of the prison. This has taken place within an overall legacy which is bound to colour any developments.

First, there is the apparently never-ending debate and confusion about what prison is for. After 1877, deterrence was the stated aim; in 1895 the Gladstone Committee Report spoke of deterrence and reform, which many still see as mutually incompatible. The intertwining of pragmatism and liberalism, and a sense of bettering people without presuming to 'change' them, has given rise to more recent statements of 'security, control and treatment', 'humane containment', and 'positive custody'. None of these embrace the whole range of attitudes that may emerge from the slightest of conversations; the point is that the prison educator is not operating in an institution with a clear-cut 'mission statement'.

This is further complicated by constant shifts in public attitudes towards crime and punishment, which, from different corners and at different times, look for reform, humane containment, retribution and punishment, and simply wishing the criminal out of sight. Also, political responsibility for penal affairs means that these attitudes are reflected in public policy.

Second, there is the shape and size of the organisation within which the Education Officer works. The Prison Act of 1877 finally removed all prisons from local authority control and established centralised responsibility. This responsibility is now vested in the Secretary of State for Home Affairs (the Home Secretary). Consequently, the Prison Department has been described as the most centralised of all our institutions. Three things flow from this.

The very size and monolithic nature of the enterprise gives rise to management and bureaucratic problems of a high order. Whilst various attempts have been made to establish regional management systems, none of these have been entirely satisfactory. Then, the combination of central responsibility and the closed nature of the prisons has a profound effect upon public attitudes – and, consequently, political attitudes towards the service. Finally, the education officer is particularly affected as he/she is essentially a locally employed officer who has to work within a massive centralised culture.

Moreover, any consideration of any aspect of the prison service has to take into account the role, attitudes and culture of the uniformed officer staff. This is a complex topic, but note needs to be taken of the responsibility of the uniformed staff for 'security and control'; their complex relationship with the specialist services in prison – psychology, chaplain, education and so on – who have different and, at times, apparently conflicting roles (and who are there for the benefit of the prisoners, not the uniformed staff); and the fact that no prison can function without the willing support of the uniformed staff.

Third, all programmes take place within the Prison Estate; and, whilst in recent years there has been a good deal of prison building – partly as a humane improvement of conditions and partly as a response to the growing prison population – many prisoners are still housed in buildings dating back to the early nineteenth century. There are the prisons which are household names; Dartmoor, Strangeways, Holloway, and so on. They are over-crowded, often insanitary, and ugly. Each has its own separate culture, accreted over many years, and whilst many have been the centre of prison riots in recent years and are universally condemned, the resource involved in the infrastructure is so great that it is difficult to conceive of the economy supporting a complete replacement programme in the foreseeable future.

Improvements are in hand, and modern replacements are being built. But it is important to realise that whilst some education programmes take place in well-equipped and custom-built surroundings, many take place in buildings constructed in an age when provisions for such specialist services in education had no part in the plan.

The problem is a dual one: there is the humane and management need to bring old accommodation up to acceptable standards. But this is aggravated by the rapidly increasing prison population and the hunt for additional accommodation. The current rate of increase is sufficient to require a new prison to be built each month. In the current restrictions on public expenditure, this not only leaves some education officers with inappropriate accommodation but also diverts available resources away from activities into capital building.

These seem to me to be the main historical strands which still permeate the prison system in England and Wales (and, to a large extent, Scotland). And more recent developments could be added – the increasing number of long-term prisoners from the 1960s onwards; the particular problems associated with remand prisoners awaiting trial; the changing nature of crime which has brought into prison a much more varied cross-section of society, both educated and uneducated. All of these have a direct bearing upon the role of the prison education officer and prison curriculum. Moreover, recent developments, both legislative and ideological in the world of education at large, promise a profound effect upon education in prisons.

The aims of education in prison

As I have implied, most 'official' statements of the aims of custody and of education within that custody tend to be bland and capable of multiple re-interpretation; at times they are mutually contradictory. This means that the prison curriculum is often shaped by a combination of the historical pressures I have referred to above and the personal vocationalism of prison education staff. A series of conversations with both education and other staff elicits the following aims – some explicit, other implicit – and most of them in combination. In other words, it is emphasis that matters rather than clearly defined, exclusive aims and objectives.

First, there is a clear and general view that access to education is a universal and human right: that imprisonment is a denial of certain freedoms, but not of the right to education. We never intend to deny prisoners food, goes the argument, so why education? This emphasises the role of prison education as an extension of the wider adult education service, and reduces our perception of the activity as being 'special'.

Second, the growth of the number of long-term prisoners has drawn increasing attention to the need, not so much to 'reform' prisoners or to prepare them functionally for return to liberty, as to maintain their mental well-being whilst serving their sentences. This argument is reinforced by the economic one; that it is cheaper to return a person to liberty who has not deteriorated to the extent that they are a further burden on public resources.

Third, the most explicit expression of reformative education emerges from the view that criminality often has functional rather than personality roots; an education programme based on this view emphasises the teaching of vocational skills with a view to subsequent employment, and the early and extensive development of adult basic education and other coping skills.

Fourth, a range of complex attitudes centre upon the role educational activity plays within the prison as an institution. It is often maintained that prisoners involved in these activities are less 'troublesome' than others, and that an establishment with an active educational and training programme tends to be more peaceful and easier to manage. Whilst most education staff wish to see a peaceful prison, if only because their own programme is less disrupted, many resent the use of education as an instrument to control, in particular as part of the rewards and punishments ethos of the prison.

Finally, a few projects are now in hand aimed specifically at behaviour modification. Some of these aim to treat sex offenders and others drug offenders, and some involve other specialist services such as psychology. Much of the work is based upon North American models, and is marked out by its explicit therapeutic aims.

As I have implied, no one education officer would profess exclusively one of those aims. This is partly the consequence of a degree of ambivalence within the Prison Service, and partly of the debate within British adult education at large about personal, functional, liberal and social aims. The point must be made that this uncertainty or tension (whichever it is) is not necessarily damaging to the service; a variety of views provides a breadth of provision and choice. And better a degree of ambivalence than a rigidly exclusive ideology.

The curriculum

It is remarkably difficult to make general statements about the educational curriculum in British prisons. Each has its unique flavour and depends upon a wide variety of local and usually practical factors. Some prisons are in urban settings, and a wider variety of part-time teaching staff is available; others are remote from such riches. For a variety of reasons, financial resources are unevenly distributed and, as has already been mentioned, some (usually modern) prisons are blessed with custom-built education space whilst others are cramped. Another factor is the nature of the prison itself; the task of the education officer in a prison inhabited by men or women at the beginning of a long sentence will be different from that in, say, an open prison where release is in sight. Again, some prisons are work-oriented whilst others are designated as training/education establishments.

But, despite these variations, the Chief Education Officer's Branch of the Prison Service is making determined efforts to establish a national curriculum. This is partly on the grounds of equity and equal opportunity for all inmates; it is partly to cope with a system which frequently transfers prisoners, either on security grounds or as they pass through their sentence. The aim is to enable prisoners to transfer into the same programme on transfer as the one they have just left.

In some ways this has become easier, as accreditation and credit transfer has become more widespread outside; nonetheless, it is a daunting task to put together a programme which meets the needs of a mobile prison population with a wide range of intellectual and personal needs. No generalisation will adequately describe the programme in any one prison. It is, though, possible to trace five main strands – the vocational; the remedial; the academic; the recreational; and (to pay note to some developments designed to treat specific areas of deviant behaviour) the 'therapeutic'.

The vocational

Less has been written about the vocational dimensions of prison vocational and training programmes than other areas. Yet it has played a significant part in prison regimes since the inception of the first course in precision engineering fitting in 1941. Although a variety of factors have brought about some changes in recent years, the activity has always been underpinned by two clear aims.

Of these, the simplest and the most often expressed is to provide prisoners with job training which will enable them to compete for satisfying and remunerative employment after release. This recognises, quite clearly, that some crime is the direct consequence of the inability to survive economically and that, given the skills, many criminals would wish to lead a crime-free life. A related and rather more subtle agenda is concerned with the relationship between vocational skills and the confidence to use those skills effectively and confidently in the work environment. Thus, many vocational programmes have also been concerned with more social attitudes and have examined simple concepts, such as time-keeping and the wider field of workplace relationships.

Until 1969, vocational training and education were seen as two separate services. In that year the administrative responsibility for the vocational programme was transferred from the Directorate of Industry and Stores to the Chief Education Officer and the two were brought together. The situation now prevails where the Prison Education Officer has management responsibility for the operation of a vocational training programme, whilst the instructors have a professional responsibility to the Home Office Prison Department. There are many ways in which the training and education programmes have come together, but vocational instructors are still civil servants, whereas 'educators' were, until recently, attached professionally to their LEA.

The vocational training programme in prisons has had to take account of a variety of factors. The first has been the necessity to achieve external recognition of awarded qualifications. Until 1950, the Prison Department awarded a Certificate of Vocational Training – in that year, certain prisoners were encouraged to attempt the City and Guilds of London Institute Craft examination. In 1971, programmes began to operate under the auspices of various Training

Boards and, more recently, to correspond with the system of National Vocational Qualifications (NVQs).

Nonetheless, problems abound. One major problem – affecting all training programmes, in prisons and outside – is that of the overall employment situation in what is a fiercely competitive situation where many industries particularly favoured in prison, such as construction and engineering, are suffering particular difficulties. Another, related, problem is the rapidly changing nature of employment to which the service must retain a flexible response. Computer training, for example, has become a central element of many programmes and is rapidly replacing the traditional emphasis on workshop training. However, a wide programme ranging from agriculture and horticulture to engineering, catering and construction is maintained.

Any serious review of the vocational training programme in the prison setting has to take account of the interface between 'training' and 'education'. It must be prepared to take any opportunity to erode that division which plagues so many areas of British adult education. Adult basic education, for example, which is provided by 'teachers', is very close in its aims to vocational training. It has a concern not only for a basic and measurable level of skill, but also for the realistic application of that skill outside prison, and for the personal and social development of the student. The world of vocational training has to be responsive to an external situation which demands transferable skills, implying an intellectual liveliness and flexibility, as much as specific skills; it also has to recognise that success at work depends as much upon surviving within a total environment as upon being able to carry out a specific task.

Organisationally, training and education have been brought closer together and progress has been made towards breaking down the cultural divide. The development of computer training is recognised as vocational and yet, for a variety of practical reasons, is perceived as being 'education'; and, as more and more instructors take advantage of training which leads them into professional teaching qualifications, so do professional relationships develop.

Remedial education

Of all areas of the prison education programme, remedial education concerned with basic literacy and numeracy has perhaps the strongest base. Not only is there a statutory duty to provide, but also everybody within the prison service recognises the extent of the problem and sees no threat in its provision. Moreover, of all the strands of prison provision, it has the longest history.

Over the last 20 years, the development of remedial education in prisons has been intertwined with the adult literacy (and the basic skills) programme developed as part of a national, public campaign, and each has benefited from the other. A sharing of part-time teaching experience has, no doubt, given a wider scope for experience developed in prison. Extensive use has been made by the prison programme of the first-rate materials developed by the public movement.

But there are essential differences.[1] First, the prisoner cannot escape exposure; educational screening on reception inevitably leads to the exposure of what may have been successfully concealed for many years. Second, there is no question of 'private' or discrete teaching situations undertaken in the home as all is public and relatively formalised. In other words, the educational setting, once rejected, is often reproduced. Finally, the student has to grapple with yet another additional dimension of complex feelings of failure, exposure and peer group pressure which already exists within the prison. So, whilst the structure may initially be easier for the education staff, the situation is often more difficult for the student and the teaching task is full of pitfalls.

Most comparative literature assumes – reasonably enough – that there is a relationship between inadequate literacy and numeracy and crime leading to imprisonment. Either one leads directly to the other, or both stem from the same source – a rejection of values instilled in educational, and other, systems. More than many other areas of the educational programme, remedial education has identifiable and assessable outcomes.

The causes of this particular inadequacy are as varied as those found outside. They range from inadequate schooling, through a number of personality problems, to specific but undiagnosed physical problems, such as poor eyesight or hearing.

There can be little doubt that this area of activity both requires and receives a high level of priority within the service. A combination of broad institutional support, clearly perceived need and measurable outcomes ensures this. At times there are problems – particularly amongst young offenders – in overcoming peer group pressure and also with student motivation. However, this latter is often secured by identifying specific student motives, ranging from vocational aspiration, coping with state bureacracy unaided, to family letter writing and academic ambition. Often – and this is no more than an impression – the need for remedial education is often greatest amongst prisoners with short sentences; and this, of course, reduces the capacity of the system to provide real, long-term help.

The academic programme

This term is used here to describe the opportunities made available within the prison for those prisoners who make the decision to embark upon a course of study (or courses) which enables them to climb a ladder of academic progression. In its most extreme (though not unheard of) form, they might proceed from basic literacy and numeracy classes *via* a range of examination boards to successful undergraduate study. One also has to take into account first the nature of the prison population where domestic murder, 'white collar' crime, and drugs-related offences ensure that many prisoners have got considerable previous educational experience and, second, the tendency in recent decades to hand down much longer sentences. This latter both increases the humanitarian need to develop extended programmes and provides the opportunity to nurture real, extended development.

Although institutional problems still, and will always, exist, a pattern of provision within prison has been developed which is remarkably close to opportunities presented outside. This involves courses leading to examination and qualification in RSA, GCSE 'O' and 'A' level, various City and Guild examinations and undergraduate courses of the Open University. Recent developments in allowing certain prisoners to attend educational colleges outside prisons on a parole basis, the use of correspondence courses and development of flexible learning programmes extend this list, as do the many local arrangements with colleges, polytechnics and universities who will send teams of teachers into prisons.

At the heart of this strand of the programme, from the point of view of both the providing institution and the student prisoner, is that it is perceived as being an extension of 'normal' non-prison life. The prison education officer, as well as feeling professional satisfaction with such developments, operates happily in this field as she/he feels less 'special' and more at one with the processes and standards of educational institutions and colleagues. The prisoner, too, usually welcomes external criteria and the sense of belonging to a wider community of students other than the prison population.

Four types of prisoner seem particularly attracted to the programmes. First, a group of previously educationally disadvantaged students will have caught the excitement of study for the first time somewhere on the lower rungs of the ladder – they will be aware, from their colleagues, of the possible progress to be made – and they will use this way of overcoming the perennial prison problem of using 'time'.

A significant second group of prisoners are previously well qualified, but have committed offences which preclude them from re-entering their previous profession on release. This group uses the programme to 'side-step', using already well-developed learning skills to move from one profession to another – accountants to statistics, lawyers to social work, teachers to commerce and so on. At the same time, such intellectual effort has a great deal to do with the intellectually lively 'surviving' a long sentence. A third group, although similar in many ways, differs because their offence does not necessarily debar them from picking up the pieces of their previous employment. In these cases, academic activity and achievement is often related to guilt and the development of that part of their personality which has not offended, and to the ability to maintain some link with the world of normality outside. A fourth group tends to be younger and to be in the situation where an offence (usually drug- or explosives-related) had interrupted an academic career. These prisoners use the academic ladder in a rather more functional way and see it as the opportunity to rescue their careers from complete disaster.

The relationship between imprisonment – particularly in the case of long-term prisoners – and the extended academic progression offered in prisons is a complex one. Examinations offer 'milestones', to see time through. Courses, tutors and programmes offer connections with the outside world. The opportunity to succeed is seen as an antidote to a community of failure – although further failure is a risk.[2] At its best, all these are illuminated by an underlying sense of intellectual discovery and excitement and the gradual development of work of high quality.

The arts and crafts

This area of prison education is perhaps the most prevalent and yet the least systematically explored. Under the banner of education it is possible for prisoners to follow a wide range of creative activities. Painting and drawing are popular activities, as are the opportunities to make a range of objects with wood, ranging from sophisticated cabinet and model-making, to carving and toy-making. Soft-toy making is also popular and instrumental classes are not uncommon. Some of the activities are cell-based, others pursued in formal or informal classes. Any tuition is paid from the education budget, whilst prisoners make a contribution to the cost of materials.

One may add to this type of activity a wide range of craft-related and artistic activity, much of which is stimulated by external agencies. A recent report[3] lists 88 different types of activity under 'Visual Arts and Crafts'; 16 under 'Literature'; 5 under 'Film'; 24 under 'Drama/Dance'; and, 29 under 'Music'. Some of these are represented in all prisons throughout the system and they take many forms. Artists visit, sometimes on an extended residence basis. Prisoners will work on artistic community projects outside the prison. The Royal Shakespere Company and other national bodies not only tour prisons, but also will work with prisoners. The variety and extent seem infinite.

The cultivation of such activities – from the relatively sophisticated to the simple process of 'making things' – is, of course, a major contribution by both institutions and prisoners to finding something positive in an environment which is always tending towards the negative. In very few cases a high level of skill is developed, in more it is seen as a satisfying – and, therefore, therapeutic – personal activity. In some it is seem as a valuable community activity which adds a different style and dimension to the prison, or develops a relationship with the community. The concepts of activity embrace and go beyond those which support similar activities in LEA adult provision.

The therapeutic programme

Significant strides have been made in recent years in developing programmes designed to treat specific forms of deviant behaviour: drug and alcohol dependency; sexual deviance; and aggressive behaviour figure large. There are occasions when this activity is lodged with the prison psychological service or the probation service and occasions when it is the consequence of fruitful collaboration, involving education. The policy of segregating sexual offenders has led to a high degree of sophisticated treatment in prisons thus designated. It varies from the rest of the prison education programme in that it is explicitly therapeutic and, of course, has different sorts of relationships with similar activities outside.

The prison education officer as adult educator

Embedded as she/he is in the prison service, the prison educator is also and essentially an adult educator. Up to 1993 this had been reflected in the employment link with the LEA and usually an appropriate college. In most cases, the new arrangements retain the link with a college or an educational body outside the prison service. The closeness of this relationship has, of course, varied. In some cases professional rapport – a sense of 'belonging' to the college – has been very strong, in others the links have been merely formal and financial.

However, it has not been possible and would not have been desirable for education in prisons to develop in one direction and external mainstream adult education in another. The arrangement was to a large extent designed to enable prison education staff to keep in touch with wider professional developments. It is to be hoped that the post–1993 contractual relationships do not isolate the educator in prison from these wider trends.

Rather like the prison service, the adult education movement has always had some difficulty in defining its purpose. Some have adhered to the aims of personal development, maintaining that education cannot work beyond the individual student. Others have indicated the social purpose of adult education, emphasising either the need to redress social injustice and the educational disadvantage of sectors of students or, more broadly, the need for an 'informed democracy' and a stable, democratic society. Futher groups have pursued the idea of community education with emphasis upon participation. All of these, with some degree of overlap, have been discussed in the light of demographic trends – for example, an increasingly ageing society – and social change – in, for example, leisure, unemployment and family structure.

In recent years the government and other central bodies have insisted that priority be given to vocational education with the national economic good in mind. Initially, many rejected this latter as functional and short-term. More recently, more sophisticated arguments have emerged denying that there is a necessary polarisation. The argument, broadly, is that specific skills training is, in the light of technological development, short-term and that truly vocational training would impart cognitive and transferable skills, as well as developing attitudinal change, enabling individuals to adjust to both social and workplace change.

This set of arguments, suitably developed, is of immediate relevance to the prison curriculum, for it is possible to move towards a model which both helps offenders to cope with the consequences – including incarceration – of their crime and to develop attitudes and transferable skills appropriate to release.

For a long time adult education, like prison education, has been marginalised. More recently, for a whole range of reasons – demographic, economic and conceptual – its importance has been realised. One effect of this move to centre stage has been an increased degree of attention, and intervention, on the part of government and other central bodies. In many ways this is gratifying, but there can be little doubt that it was more comfortable in the margins.

The impression is that prison education is going through a similar process. Tolerated, and at times encouraged, it carried neither the over-riding priority of security and control nor the professional 'rights' of other specialisms such as medical care. But – helped to a certain extent by the movement outside – it is now seen more clearly as contributing to the 'dynamic regime' and the 'active sentence'/'prison' called for by both the Inspectorate of Prisons and the Home Secretary amongst others. Also, its bearing upon other areas of the prison regime is more clearly perceived. Again, there has to be some concern that, in some prisons, one effect of the post-1993 arrangements has been to remove the Education Officer – now clearly funded *via* another route – from the prison governor's management committee.

The inevitable result of this is – and will increasingly be – that prison education is much more widely discussed and more carefully examined than before. This is not too comfortable, but is an inevitable stage in reaching a position where education's full potential is recognised. The important thing is – and it should be part of a developing professionalism – that prison educators should have their own philosophy and their case developed before these challenges have to be met head-on.

One of the pressures upon adult education is towards an increasing functionalism. This is in part the consequence of governmental belief that the process can – as I indicate above – make a contribution to the nation's economic health. But it is also reflected in central demands for measurable outcomes in return for the expenditure of public money. The consequence is twofold: first, patterns of funding are based upon student numbers, retention rates and the like; and, second, courses are directed much more towards identifiable awards and qualifications.

This is already happening in prison education and the process will, no doubt, accelerate under the new contractual system. This seems to give rise to two problems. The first is that prison education has existed for a long time not only as a producer of measurable outcomes but, to a large extent, upon the strength of its less tangible products. The second is that there is always the danger of claiming much more than can be 'proved'. This latter, of course, is what has undermined the 'treatment' model. Not so much that it could be shown to be ineffective, but that it was impossible to tease out the effects of a particular 'treatment' from any other part of a prison sentence. It is important that work be done – from within the prison education service – to establish what the profession itself has as appropriate measures.

It becomes increasingly difficult to say what 'adult education' is and to make a case on its behalf. But as one looks past the general term and identifies specific areas of work, then the case is more readily accepted. Adult Basic Education is perhaps the prime example of this; but one could add programmes and projects directed at other target groups – minority ethnic groups, the elderly, and so on – which have had conspicuous success. It is also noticeable that few professionals these days claim to be 'adult educators'; rather, they profess a specialist field.

Is it possible that the same process is developing within prison education? One is more and more aware of increasing interest in programmes with specific targets and of the diminishing meaning of a generic term, such as 'prison education' in this context of different groupings of prisons and prisoners, each with different and special needs.

Conclusion: the future

Of the many changes crowding in upon the Prison Service in recent years, several seem to be supportive of the role of the Prison Education Officer. Several of these changes have emerged from within the prison service itself. Both the May Report[4] and the Woolf Report[5] made positive comments and recommendations about the part education plays, and could play, within the prison service. Whilst the government has not been able to support all the recommendations to the extent that many would have wished, many of the points raised have chimed in with a re-appraisal of management styles within the Home Office Prison Department and in individual establishments.

The concept of the integrated regime is being developed. Whereas in the past, the life of the prisoner has been usually fragmented – domestic life on the wings, work, education, physical activity and exercise, and association elsewhere – considerable efforts are now being made to develop creative links between these elements.

In the long term, this should raise the status of education; instead of being a separate and, at times, isolated series of activities, viewed as a process, it could begin to inform all areas of the regime. A review of the educational curriculum will not only weld together different strands within the explicit education programme, but also, taken in its widest sense, begin to move towards the creation of the total educational regime with all that it implies for individuals' perceptions of their roles and relationships within the prison.

This is already reflected in the management arrangements of many prisons. Two features dominated previous arrangements: first, the dominant, central influence of the Home Office; and second, the individual authority of the prison governor running several, often quite separate, functions within the prison.

The Home Office has now devolved many responsibilities and budgetary decisions from the centre. This has coincided with more developed thinking about the intergrated regime and has led to a management style whereby the governor is, in effect, the Chairperson of a management committee on which all sectional interests are represented.

The ultimate effect of this, as far as education is concerned, would only have been seen when the effect of the presence of education staff on such committees was appraised. No doubt, this would have varied from prison to prison and depended very much upon personal dynamics. Nonetheless, it presented an opportunity for the prison service to reassess exactly what it means by 'education' and for individuals to reconsider their curriculum and to relate in a different fashion to the rest of prison. However, the recent contracting–out system may have lost this opportunity.

In parallel with this is the development of the 'negotiated sentence'. This concept is informed by the idea that any sentence should be 'useful' and that both prisoner and prison service should be fully aware of their relationship and mutual obligations. The prisoner is invited to plan his or her sentence in col-laboration with prison authorities; both then enter into a 'contract'. If educa-tion, for example, plays a significant part in that 'contract' then its position becomes significant. It becomes part of an assurance made by the prison service – and prison education has always had a low priority in such matters as initial dispersal and transfers – and it develops a higher profile in the prisoner's concept of his or her sentence.

The Woolf Report, in particular, placed strong emphasis not only on educational activities, but also upon community links, and both danger and damage were seen in the traditional isolation of the prison community from the world outside. Of all activities within prison, the education service has the strongest links with the community. Within the overall concept that education within the prison is a natural extension of education without, there are already extensive local links as part-time teachers – and in some cases outside classes – visit prisons. External education and examining bodies are used and temporary release from prison to follow courses becomes increasingly available.

The position of the Prison Education Officer – or 'Co-ordinator', as she/he in now known – is as delicately balanced in 1997 as is the service she/he represents. Budgetary cuts get deeper each year, as increasing stresses bear down on other areas of the prison service. The 1993 contractual arrangements seem to have produced a situation of some ambivalence as far as their standing in the prison is concerned. Moreover, there seems to be increasing uncertainty amongst both public and politicians as to what prisons are for and what imprisonment should be like.

The demand is increasingly for measurable outcomes as their vocationalism tells them that their major outcomes are not measurable. Their lot is one of uncertainty and, at times, frustration and isolation. It is to their enormous credit that lively and imaginative programmes survive.

Increasingly, adult education is widening its boundaries to recognise different forms of informal learning. The development of processes such as the accreditation of prior learning (APL) and the accreditation of prior experiential learning (APEL) is a symptom of this, and an attempt to recognise formally the fact that learning takes place in a wide variety of settings – the home, the workplace – as well as in the classroom.

Applied to the prison setting, this would seem to imply that the education programme is one special form of learning within a wide variety of other learning experiences. For a whole range of reasons – not least to perceive a broad unity of purpose – it will be necessary to be sensitive to the part formal education plays in relationship to other learning opportunities presented within the prison.

Notes

[1] As pointed out by Grainge and Kemp, 'Remedial Education in Prison', in W Forster (ed), *Prison Education in England and Wales,* NIACE, 1981.

[2] This is explored further in *The Higher Education of Prisoners,* by W Forster, University of Leicester, 1976.

[3] *Arts Activites in Prisons,* by A Peaker and J Vincent, Home Office, 1989.

[4] *Report of the Committee to Inquire into the United Kingdom Prison Service* under Mr Justice May, HMSO, 1979.

[5] *Prison Disturbances April 1990,* Report of an Inquiry by the Rt Hon Lord Justice Woolf and His Honour Judge Stephen Tumim, HMSO, 1990.

Chapter Five

The French prison education system: a regional structure

J Duprey-Kennedy, Proviseur, Direction Régionale des Services Penitentiaires, Strasbourg and member of EPEA Steering Committee

Historical context and current issues

The idea of prison education only started to emerge from the end of the 18th century. At the beginning of the 19th century, a moral, religious and work-related education was recommended in the rehabilitation of young offenders. But it was only after the Second World War that a director of Prison Administration incorporated work and education into his reform of the prison system to aid rehabilitation.

From then on things accelerated. From 1950, teachers became involved, intially voluntarily. In 1964, 13 teachers were appointed, their role defined by the penal procedure code and recognised by the Ministry for National Education. They were responsible for an unskilled prison population, the objective being to teach fundamental skills – reading, writing and arithmetic – and to prepare students for the first diploma, the Certificate in Primary Studies. Later the College Certificate would be taught in certain establishments.

During 1968, a college structure was established at the prison in Fleur-Mérogis. The idea of a college within a prison grew with the desire to help certain prisoners gain the *baccalauréat* and a university education. This college was recognised in 1985 with the appointment of a head and the programme was extended. It led to the opening of prison colleges around Strasbourg, Lille and Marseille between 1988 and 1990.

From 1985, the Ministry for National Education and the Ministry for Justice led an enquiry into the benefits of prison education and into the type of structure which had been put in place to implement this education. The negotiations led to a signed agreement in 1995, creating Regional Educational Units which, from 1997, have been required to correspond to the nine prison centres in the area.

The Regional Educational Unit, directed by a co-ordinator, organises all levels of teaching: primary; secondary; and eventually university level. It establishes links with vocational trainers, associations who teach – literacy skills,

French as a foreign language, and so on – and public or private bodies for correspondence courses.

Table 5.1: 1995 National Statistics

Prison population on one day	Annual rate	Number of Students	Teaching hours
53,413	98,630	224,469	8,747

Aims of the system

The first objective of prison education is the rehabilitation of the prisoner: to use the sentence time to acquire the minimum necessary skills for general life; to draw up a work requirement; fill in papers; and, to understand forms. The fight against illiteracy is therefore a priority. For those more capable, the aim is to help them obtain diplomas and formal qualifications which improve their chances of finding work.

However, for some prisoners, before speaking about reintegration it is first of all necessary to talk about integration. Education, at whatever level, allows reflection of oneself and reformation of an individual who is confronted by rules, work, and a goal to achieve. Education allows one to reconcile school and culture which are often synonyms for failure and rejection. Reforming the individual helps to combat subsequent offending and provides constructive channels for energies in the prison. For short- and long-term sentences, prison education seeks to protect society and the maximum effort must be made to prevent young offenders from re-offending.

Structure and management

Many different bodies are involved in the delivery of prison education. Within the framework of the Regional Education Unit, the teachers provided by the Ministry for Education deal with the initial training. These are primary and secondary studies, which lead to diplomas taken in schools and colleges – Certificat de Formation Générale, Brevet, Baccalauréat. They work in prisons where an education centre is available for prisoner students. Examinations are organised on site by teachers who establish links with external examination centres for marking and oral work.

In conjunction with associations like GENEPI (The Students' Association of Voluntary Aid for Prisoners) or others who specialise in the care of immigrants, supporting activities – such as tutorials or French courses – are provided.

Collaboration also takes place with the vocational training body which delegates the preparation of the *Certificat d'aptitude professionelle* (diploma obtained after vocational training) or *Brevets d'études professionels* (Certificates in Vocational Studies) to public or private organisations.

Teachers are at the centre of the internal structure. They include tutors, social workers and visitors to the prison. Externally there is the Centre for Information and Training and the National Agency for Employment, which work towards the rehabilitation of the prisoner. These organisations carry out different types of work and are involved in areas such as library services and correspondence courses.

The various service providers are managed by the Department of Prison Services. This department comprises four bodies with a director in overall charge: the education action unit (initial training for national education); the vocational training unit (training qualifications, public and private organisations); the social education unit (libraries, associations); and the work and employment unit (workshop and technical instruction). The Department, under the Regional Director, organises regional training projects.

Course aims

Courses are organised in flexible modules to allow the prisoner to organise his or her own project in relation to their sentence period and their education level. The teaching is designed to take students from assessment into various appropriate local training schemes. Fee-paying vocational training can be for a short time – several months – and may lead to a recognised qualification (credit points). Intial non-fee-paying training is longer when involving a diploma. Short modules of several weeks exist, however, with certain precise objectives to reach. Certain training schemes are carried out in conjuction with external enterprises to prepare students for their departure. In the case of a prisoner being transferred, centralisation across regions, indeed nationally, allows a prisoner to follow a course that he or she has begun.

Current perspectives and problems

Education faces a number of diffculties, which fall under two main headings: difficulties related to a prison population; and enviromental difficulties.

Difficulties related to a prison population

The majority of prisoners come from underprivileged backgrounds. They are in the first place anti-school and anti-society, and against constraints upon them. It is important to adapt, indeed create, an education which attracts and maintains their interest.

Prisoners often have the attitude of consumers and do not always come to the courses to learn, but rather to take advantage of a group, to have contact with the outside world. They therefore invest little, especially in terms of written work. Course attendance is not always consistent, it depends upon their pre-occupations and morale.

The variety of ages, nationalities and cultures make the task of teaching difficult and make it necessary to have small groups – a maximum of 12.

Environmental difficulties

The changing prison population makes teaching groups very unstable, with changes being all the greater with young offenders, making longer training courses difficult. This instability is exacerbated by the constraints on prison life – visits, various meetings – and by the security demands which can prevent certain prisoners following courses. Finally the over-population of prisons leads to bad working conditions in cells.

With too many demands upon the tutor – such as that of confidant – teachers themselves are at risk of losing sight of their principal aim. They must strive to avoid this at all costs.

Staff

With regard to national education, teachers work voluntarily. Their application is considered by a commission and they are recruited by interview. The teachers are generally qualified to work in the area of educational difficulties. They are under the authority of their education inspectors and of the manager of the unit.

In each prison, a teacher is the local person in charge, dealing with the daily problems and organising the teaching structure under the control of the regional manger. The teachers brought in on the second degree structures often teach in schools and colleges and make up their extra hours in prisons.

These full- or part-time teachers are responsible to a regional manager who co-ordinates the prison teaching programmes and establishes a regional educational structure in accordance with the regional training programme for the regional management of prison services. This manager, who is a head of a school or director of a specialist establishment, is responsible to both the Rector for National Education and the Regional Director for Justice. Regular annual meetings are held to maintain organisation at both the regional and national level. The signed agreement between the two Ministries, other than defining the role of prison education and of the manager at the centre of the prison, deals with financial costs. Staff are paid by the Ministry for National Education whilst the Ministry for Justice meets the running costs of the service.

Recent significant developments

The creation of regional educational bodies corresponding to nine prison centres stemming from negotiations between the two Ministries – National Education and Justice – demonstrates the interest expressed by the authorities in prison education and is laid out in a formal agreement and training policy document. The appointment of a manager, to direct the regional management of prison services and the rehabilitation and probation department, shows the role played by education in the rehabilitation and positive development of the prisoner.

Table 5.2 Growth in prison population and related educational developments

	1990	1991	1992	1993	1994	1995
Prison population at 1 January	45,420	49,105	50,115	50,742	52,551	53,935
Level I	13411	13009	13794	14945	16683	17036
Level II Stage i	2034	2688	2907	4131	5250	4928
Stage ii & BAC Preparation	287	251	227	317	684	2269
Higher Education	156	237	182	195	259	319
Prisoners in correspondence courses	2189	2021	1763	1651	1520	1613
Total in Classes	15888	16185	17110	19588	22876	24552

Table 5.3 Participation in examinations

	1990	1991	1992	1993	1994	1995
CEP, CFG						
Candidates	2518	1687	1863	1921	2124	2016
Successful	1945	1357	1537	1651	1765	1691
DNC, CAP, BEP						
Candidates	209	193	214	224	245	252
Successful	112	88	122	133	137	178
BACCALAUREAT						
Candidates	66	73	40	73	70	67
Successful	39	46	21	40	38	42
ESEU						411
Candidates	142	141	74	93	119	134
Successful	63	85	41	53	60	79
HIGHER EDUCATION						
Candidates	49	38	63	84	122	72
Successful	36	26	27	59	83	60

Table 5.4 Vocational activities

	1990	1991	1992	1993	1994	1995
Non-participants	24423	26605	27229	27607	29006	N/A
Receiving pay	19490	20666	20884	20657	21234	21920
Prison industries	1820	1564	1448	1364	1325	1250
General occupations	6266	6668	5910	6941	6892	6862
Agencies	8380	8797	8946	8395	9261	9637
Partial release	780	901	779	779	822	1431
Vocational training	2244	2625	2801	3177	2934	2740

Education policy and its translation into action in penal institutions in the Federal Republic of Germany

Klaus-D. Vogel, Head of Pedagogical Service, Berlin-Moabit Remand Prison

This chapter presents the education policy and its translation into action in penal institutions in the Federal Republic of Germany. Initially, it deals with the problem that, although certain delinquent traits of character often correlate significantly with shortcomings in education, education alone is no guarantee against delinquency. Education is therefore permanently under pressure to justify itself with reports of success, in order to be acknowledged as being a meaningful component part of the execution of justice. A compendium of the historical development of a pedagogically-oriented execution of justice from the 16th Century to the present day outlines the growing recognition of a right to education, one which also applies to the imprisoned. This is made unmistakably clear in the European Principles on Execution of Justice of the Council of Europe, or in its Recommendations No R (89) 12 concerning Further Education within the Penal System of 1989, but also indirectly in the German National Law on the Execution of Justice of 1976.

The depiction of the concrete tasks and organisational structures of the departments of education and the teaching profession in the German state penal system gives an overview of the variety of educational possibilities characterising the present situation in penal institutes in the federally-administered and governed states of Germany. These possibilities range from elementary and basic education to preparation for secondary school graduation, the attainment of professional qualifications and even university courses. In this chapter I also take into account and give examples of the practical basic framework of the teaching work and methods of study in the German state penal institutions.

At the end of this chapter, the problems and shortcomings currently being faced in penal institutional education in Germany are discussed, as are the non-uniform assessment of the necessary extent of educational courses on offer to prisoners. This is followed by a section on the difficult financial situation and personnel problems especially in the so-called New States of Germany and their consequences. Finally I discuss changes in the target groups of institutional education and the further conceptual, curricular and methodologcal developments which these will make necessary.

Education and punishment

Educationalists in the German penal system find themselves confronted over and over again with a seemingly insoluble problem. The problem is the fact that the majority of prisoners have obviously received an insufficient education, one which is clearly related to the socialisation specific to their social stratum as well as to their disposition for delinquency. However, the educational possibilities on offer in the penal institutions have not been able to show any significant successes as far as resocialisation is concerned. After the generally optimistic expectations of the 1980s concerning the resocialising effects of pedagogical intervention in the penal process, current criminological research reveals a degree of scepticism concerning the tendency of released prisoners to commit subsequent offences. The successful reintegration of discharged prisoners appears rather to correlate significantly with such personal characteristics as the age at time of and duration of, registration as a criminal, as well as the social environment. It correlates less with the intervention of the penal system. Professional integration alone seems to aid them to make a break with their career as a delinquent (Baumann, 1996: 74).

Put simply, this means that education alone is no guarantee against delinquency! Thus, penal institutional education is under permanent pressure to legitimise itself. It finds itself having to justify its right to continued existence as a meaningful component part of the penal system, by providing figures on such things as the number of course participants, the school exams passed and professional qualifications obtained. The problem is that, according to popular opinion, prisoners or law-breakers are to be punished and must perhaps evenpay for their sins. A small book, well worth reading, written by a minister from Berlin about his experiences in the large Tegel Men's Prison, Berlin, which has more than 1,300 prisoners, is ironically entitled *Now Expiate Your Sins* (See, 1983). Participation in schooling and educational measures, however, is not considered to be arduous enough to live up to the supposed penitential nature of the punishment. First and foremost, the prisoners have duties: namely to work for an average of 10 DM per day; to co-operate in achieving the aim of their punishment, ie their reintegration; not to impair the order and peace of the institution; and to obey the directives of the public employees of the institution. The following may be regarded as the rights of the imprisoned:

- the right to health care and hygiene;
- spiritual welfare;
- privacy and the retention of contact with the family;
- the polite form of address 'Sie';
- the principle of equal treatment;

- the lodging of complaints and verification of decisions of the authorities in court; and lastly,
- the right to preparatory measures for release from prison with a view to social reintegration into freedom, including measures such as aid in the search for a flat with job placement and any meaningful training or educational measures which might be necessary to this end. However, all of these rights are in general perceived by the institutional administration as being burdensome and unreasonable, since they are often the cause of work which is considered to be unproductive. This is also often work which in many cases requires the deployment of personnel which is at the best of times in great shortage and which in some cases may reveal some of the shortcomings of the penal concept.

Even today, therefore, the legal claim of prisoners to education and training is still not indisputable in the modern German penal system. At the fore is the discussion of the question of what volume of education is necessary, and to what extent it can be justified to and financed by the public.[1] In practice, however, this argument is usually supported by a trivial criminological hypothesis that more education and training could of course enable those concerned to commit new crimes. The formerly illiterate criminal could become a counterfeiter. The newly-trained locksmiths could become safecrackers; the computer expert a dealer in pirate copies. The only things which can fend off these accusations are appropriate explanations and social commitment. To this end, a look at the historical development of the goals of the penal system as well as the present legal basis in the Federal Republic of Germany supplies us with the most important facts.

Historical development of the aims of the penal system

Education is just *one* aspect of several different aims in the penal process. But it was not until the Enlightenment in the 18th Century that it first became significancant. Since the time of the Babylonians, imprisonment had basically served the purpose, not of punishment, but of keeping the perpetrator behind bars until his sentence ended. So it was more or less a kind of detention while awaiting trial, or detention while awaiting execution (Kette, 1991: 6). What followed was usually execution but could be physical punishment: from corporal punishment to public denunciation; from blinding to the severing of limbs; burning; hanging; or breaking on the wheel or decapitation. Only in the case of perpetrators who were of the elevated status of nobility or clergy was the punishment of imprisonment actually carried out, and even this was only out of a certain fear of killing these people (Kaiser *et al*, 1991: 34). It was not until the 13th Century that the prison sentence – but even here without any ideas of education – became a part of the jurisdiction of the growing cities alongside physical punishment and execution.

In 1532 imprisonment became a law of the Empire in the Constitutio Criminalis Carolina Karl V, the first Common Criminal Law with a code of criminal procedure (Heuer, 1977: 26). The idea of an educational prison sentence appeared first towards the end of the 16th Century as the result of general social reforms. The cities began to reorganise their systems of supply and control towards the end of the Middle Ages (Walter, 1991: 24). All sorts of things such as the impoverishment of the rural population; uprooting processes; the Crusades and those who returned from them; vagrancy; beggars and vagabonds; and prostitution – all these things were a burden to the community and required more flexible solutions than the Carolina could provide. The new idea, which corresponded with the growing mercantilism, was education to an orderly way of life and to the capability of earning their own bread, through work and strict discipline. Work which could be institutionally organised, in most cases simple handicrafts eg textile manufacture, was already present in the trading centres. It was in this way then, that the idea of improving and resocialising criminals through a prison sentence was born, an idea which even went so far as to fulfil economically profitable ends. Houses of work and discipline for men came into being in 1555 in Bridewell, England (House of Corrections) and in 1595 in Amsterdam, as well as the Spinnhaus for women in 1597. Also, following this, a number of penal institutions were founded in the larger cities of Germany – such as Nuremberg in 1588; Bremen in 1609; Lübeck in 1613; Hamburg in 1622. However, in these cases, the basic idea was that hard labour was of great educational worth, and that the product should, if necessary, be guaranteed by the use of brutal means of coercion. In an ordinance of 1682 concerning the Munich Prison it was written:

> Here ill-bred children, naughty and thoughtless people, lazy farm hands and farm maids, evil and slow servants and bricklayers, lazy odd-job men and part-time labourers should be kept, to sum up, everyone who is up to no good, or who survives by begging and idleness, so that their lives can be improved, or so that they can be brought to a place where they will no longer trouble or mislead other people . . . so that after being weighed down with iron and chains they can live with little nutrition and in bad living conditions doing hard labour, under the whip and strict discipline, or so that they can be punished or humiliated in some other way (Eisenhardt, 1978: 31).

It was not until the 19th Century that the prison sentence became widely accepted as the normal form of criminal punishment. Under the influence of the Enlightenment, its goals increasingly became subject to reforms through the work of committed pioneers: above the gate of the first reform school, The House of Bad Rogues, founded by Pope Clemens IX in San Michele near Rome in 1703, the following motto can be read:

It is not sufficient to hem in the law-breakers by punishing them. Rather we must make them into honest men through education (Kette, 1991: 7)

The prison minister Heinrich Wagnitz wrote the first analysis of the situation of the penal system in Germany in 1791, and demanded improvements:

Everywhere, people are becoming more aware of human rights, and some time it will be the turn of the imprisoned, too, and the princes who have up until now not done so, will some time deem even these people worthy of their fatherly care (Wagnitz, 1791: 111)

Other men of the clergy such as Theodor Fliedner (1800–1864) and Johann-Heinrich Wiechern (1808–1881) devoted their work to establishing spiritual welfare in prison and to the education of the imprisoned. The Rhine-Westfalia Prison Association, founded by Fliedner in 1826, employed teachers for the penal system. So it is no surprise to hear that prison teachers were often assigned to clergymen as assistants, and often had to play the organ at the service on Sundays (Walter, 1991: 165)

In the Rawitscher Reglement of 1835 which had, with some amendments, been valid for the whole of Prussia until 1902, the following was denoted as an addition to the religious education:

If a prisoner is so retarded in his knowledge that, according to the discretion of the clergy, he had taken part in this educational course (religious education) without even the slightest success, then he will be prepared for it in advance by an elementary teacher (Krebs, 1974: 51).

In a statistical survey of the level of education among criminals with subsequent records in Prussian prisons between 1894 and 1897, the percentage of illiterates was given as being eight per cent, while the percentage of prisoners with unsatisfactory elementary education was given as being 48 per cent (Leuss, 1903: 239). Even if a policy on education and learning within the penal system did slowly gain ground in the second half of the 19th Century, it remained to be justified on moral and ethical grounds. Several different criminal law reformers did try to de-emotionalise the issue, as well as to show the connections with social developments in society. For example, the director of the Stade Royal Penal Institution 1866 made the following comment on the question as to why there were so many representatives of the lower social strata in the penal institutions:

This can be said in few words: it is the pressure of social circumstances which turns men of the lower classes into criminals so disproportionately often . . . What is more we must add to these dangerous circumstances the following: poverty, bad example, direct misleading, unsatisfactory upbringing, unsatisfactory schooling, lack of judgement, superstition, unclear legal concepts etc. We who belong to the educated class, must admit that it is not of our own doing that we have been able to preserve our respectability. Our pathway through life was smoothed out for us right from the very beginning. (Heine, 1866: 14).

Even until after the founding of the Empire, the sovereign penal authorities as well as other political centres of gravity in the Empire stood in the way of the wider acceptability of these approaches to reform. It was not until the era of the Weimar Republic, when the juvenile court act came into force in 1923, that the policy on treatment and education was able, at least in theory, to gain acceptance. Even for detention while awaiting trial, educational arrangements were made:

> *It is not right to leave the educational work up to a prison sentence which might never even happen. On the first day of detention while awaiting trial, the pedagogical momentum must at all costs appear at the centre of attention, otherwise the danger could arise that the young people will deteriorate instead of being improved by the prison environment (Strube, 1931:53).*

The following is taken from a 1931 account of the Berlin-Moabit remand prison. The targets are defined by the head teacher of the institution as being social recuperation and elevation of the prisoners towards their integration into society, and he summarises:

> *Here, we endeavour, against all odds, from the moment of the prisoner's arrival to the time of his release, to live up to the modern standards of the execution of justice, to learn to comprehend, understand and value the inner man on the basis of his biological structure, to strengthen him in his will, so that he is filled with desire and warmth, so that he may belong to the environment of his past and so that he may, once again, be a brother to his fellow-man outside (Strube, 1931:124).*

The School Rules For The Penal Institutions Of The Administration Of Justice in Prussia from 1924 describes the task of the institutional schools as follows: ' . . . to raise the moral standards of the prisoners, to give them mental stimulation, and to fill in gaps in their knowledge'. Another Prison Act drafted in 1927 by the Imperial Minister of Justice, Gustav Radbruch, had also been influenced by educational policy, and understood the prisoners, first and foremost, as holders of rights (Walter, 1991: 30f).

However, before it became possible to put these socially just and humanitarian attempts at reform into practice, the tyranny of the National Socialists wrecked their newly-made progress. An inhuman justice was followed by inhuman conditions of imprisonment (Ortner 1988: 36). The elements of security and deterrence came once again to the fore. Towards the end of the war, resocialisation gave way to defence of the front, and of course served the purpose of the mobilisation of the final forces (Kette, 1991: 9).

After the end of the war, the work had to start more or less from scratch again. The 1950s were characterised by the desolate condition of the buildings, overcrowding and a lack of politically clean personnel, thus leaving conceptual problems at first unconsidered. The rule of law was the need of the moment, so that it was not until the 1960s that an enthusiasm for reform gave rise to a new optimism concerning treatment. This came after many of those from the war generation had gone into retirement and had been replaced by qualified employees who had been educated in a more liberal and democratic way. They were supported in addition by psychologists and sociologists. An early result of this new era of the execution of justice in the Federal Republic of Germany was the current Prison Act which came into force on 1 January 1977.

It should also be mentioned that the penal system in the former German Democratic Republic (GDR) can also claim to having had its own resocialisation concept, whereby prisoners were trained or received further education in order to reintegrate them into society. The Prison Act and the Reintegration Act of the GDR of 1977 were, of course, directed towards socialist education through discipline and labour.[2]

Since German reunification, the penal system in the so-called new German States of the former GDR is now being run on the basis of the reconciliation agreement of 31 August 1990 according to the legal provisions of the system in the old German States.

Penal education requirements and the current legal basis

So, what are the educational goals which justify the present penal system in the Federal Republic of Germany? What educational laws exist for the benefit of prisoners in the Federal Republic of Germany?

At the end of the 20th Century, the state of the education system for prisoners has changed little in comparison with the beginning in 19th Century Prussia. Depending on which research results are used, it has been determined that between 30 per cent and 50 per cent of prisoners have left school without any qualifications, and that at least 50 per cent have not completed any practical training courses (Cornel, 1994: 344). Between three and ten per cent of the prisoners could either not read and write at all, or could only do so inadequately (Vogel, 1992: 112). Approximately one quarter of the prisoners have considerable difficulties in mastering these skills (Schins et al, 1994: 157). If we argue from the premise, and we may justifiably do so, that basic education and professional training are factors which are of great importance in the development of an individual, and thus also in the reintegration of released prisoners, then the need for such educational opportunities in the penal system is quite obvious.

Paragraphs 37 and 38 of the German Prison Act take this state of affairs into account to some extent. Here, training and further educational measures are not only given the same value and status as, but even have a certain edge over, the normal allocation of jobs.

Paragraph 37 states:

(1) Work, occupational work therapy, training and further education serve, in particular, the purpose of imparting, obtaining and nurturing the capabilities needed to carry out a profession after the prisoner's release . . .

(3) Suitable prisoners shall be given the opportunity of learning a profession, taking further professional training or retraining courses, or taking part in other educational or further educational measures . . .

Paragraph 38 states:

(1) For suitable prisoners who have not yet obtained secondary modern school qualifications, either lessons in the subjects leading to secondary level qualifications or teaching equivalent to that of a special school are to be provided . . .

(2) Lessons are to take place during working hours.[3]

When released from the obligation to work, according to Paragraph 44, prisoners who take part in training and further education courses will receive financial educational assistance on the same lines as their earnings. This is intended to avoid any conflict of interests between earning money through employment and taking further education. The provisions for the execution of juvenile court sentences are adequate although again, somewhat irritatingly, the law speaks of 'suitable prisoners' to whom 'opportunities for professional training . . . or participation in other training or further educational measures' as well as in lessons should be given. But the teachers always come to the conclusion that, in many cases, the suitability of the prisoners for training and education must first be created by giving them the necessary basic education. The ability to read and write is just a partial qualification alongside things such as power of concentration and staying power, the ability to order and organise things, powers of verbal expression, methods of effective problem solving and planning, and so on. In practice, therefore, the educational work is more difficult than it appears to be in the small print of the legal texts. Taking lessons with a view to obtaining secondary school qualifications as well as professional training, are viewed for the most part as meaningful ways of organising time in imprisonment and as meaningful methods of resocialisation. In some individual cases, A Level (Abitur) or even university level correspondence courses are also seen as meaningful. Literacy training is also recognised as being meaningful, for this reason: everybody should at least be able to read and write!

However, recognition of the fact that primary and secondary education is more than just reading and writing can by no means be seen as an established and accepted fact. The need for the following areas of knowledge should be recognised:

- sufficient knowledge of mathematics – as far as I know, about two thirds of prisoners underachieve in this area;
- a basic political education is not just important, but a prerequisite for learning to live together with others in society in an autonomous and socially responsible way;

- learning to act in a competent way within a society, being able to interact, to criticise or to co-operate;
- being able to cope with certain practical aspects of life, such as doing tax returns, filling in insurance claims and pay-by-instalment contracts; and
- the practical mastery of modern technologies in the domain of data processing and telecommunications.

All this requires the intensive support of all teachers involved with penal education. Only then will the Federal German penal system perhaps be more successful in fulfilling its ultimate goal, as stated in Paragraph 2 of the Prison Act, namely: to enable the prisoners to create a life without crime for themselves in the future, where they are aware of their social responsibility.

Penal educators receive notional support in their endeavours. However, this is not so much from the Federal German penal system regulations – which tend to be based on a stereotyped picture of the 'suitable' and motivated course participant, who can be educated or trained without any great professional endeavours – but more from international recommendations. Such recommendations as those of the ministerial conference of the European Parliament No R (89) 12 on Further Education within the Penal System (1989) appeal to a fundamental right to education according to the UN Convention on Human Rights (1948), which says in Article 26 (1): 'Every person has a right to education'. They also appeal to the 'European Convention on the Protection of Human Rights and Basic Liberties' of the European Parliament (1950), which makes comprehensive demands for prisons to be equipped with a broad range of educational offers for all prisoners. The convention goes on to demand the orientation of the choice of educational courses on offer towards the development of the complete man, while taking into consideration his social, economic and cultural living conditions (Council of Europe, 1990: 17). This is unlike the Federal German Prison Act, which interprets education as meaning the right of prisoners to resocialisation through 'training' so that the individual is able to work and earn an income (Hoffmeyer, 1979: 263). Here a wider approach to basic education is postulated, which is more able to live up to the requirements of the modern penal system. The European Principles on the Penal System of the European Parliament (1987) state with regard to the task of education:

> *66. It is of the utmost importance that the penal system is organised and operated in such a way that . . . the prisoners are offered the possibility of developing their abilities and thus to improve their prospects for reintegration into society after their release . . .*
> *80. For prisoners with particular problems such as illiteracy or those who cannot do arithmetic, special development programmes should be offered (Federation of Public Employees in the Penal System of Germany, 1995:14)*

So, what is needed is a comprehensive education programme. The penal system in Federal Germany, however, still has a long way to go before it will be able to realise this goal.

Structuring of educational work

Conceptional and organisational conditions

In the 357 Federal German detention centres[4] with, in 1993, an average of 64,071 prisoners, there were 413 teachers employed on a full-time basis; 1,127 social workers and 435 psychologists, sociologists and educationalists.[5] These full-time members of the teaching staff plan, organise and make all practical arrangements for the educational services on offer in the penal institutions. They do this according to the specific administrative regulations of their State, as well as on the basis of their own analyses of need or areas of emphasis. The basic federalised structure of the Federal Republic of Germany prevents a uniform concept of education and educational structure from being introduced to penal institutions nationwide. Some States have, in some cases, very strictly formulated, administrative guidelines, which describe both the goals of penal educational work as well as the assignment of duties to the penal educational-ists, eg North Rhine – Westfalia, Rheinland-Pfalz, Saarland and Brandenburg, while other States do not. Some of the terms of reference for the Ministry of Justice of Rhineland-Pfalz are listed below.

Within the framework of the penal system, the following particular areas are the duty of the specialised department for education:

- educational support of the prisoners;
- participation in the planning of the penal system and the treatment of the prisoners;
- supporting the director of the institution in educational matters, training, further education and advising the employees of the institution . . .

The educational support of the prisoners includes in particular the following:

- planning, development and extrapolation of educational proposals in keeping with requirements;
- giving of lessons;
- carrying out examinations and assessments;
- giving advice and support in matters of schoollevel, professional training and further education (Ministry of Justice of Rhineland-Pfalz, 1986: 1).

One thing that the educational departments of the penal institutions have in common is that they are oriented towards the traditional school qualifications of the Federal German education system, as well as towards the uniform profes-sional training. They also adhere to the relevant curricula and examination regulations schemes of the educational authorities or trade corporations and Chambers of Industry and Commerce. However, the extent to which educational measures are actually initiated in each of the penal institutions and the extent to which the educationalists are actually involved in the treatment of the prisoners is dependent on all sorts of different factors. They include the specific needs of the institution; the status and reputation of the department in charge; financial and personnel resources, the political concepts; the support given and interest shown on the part of the political decision-makers in the supervisory authorities; and last but not least, the personal commitment of the educationalists themselves.

This results in an area of responsibility for the educationalists which is complex but also non-uniform. Depending on their job and status, each of them fulfils one or more of the following tasks:

- planning, provision and evaluation of school-level, professional and recreational educational schemes;
- giving lessons to prisoners, but also within the staff development programme of the public employees of the institution;
- participation in personality assessment of the prisoners as well as in planning individual educational strategies;
- co-operation with the external municipal educational establishments, administrative authorities and supporting institutions or individuals;
- organisation and co-ordination of cultural events (theatre, music, sports tournaments, films, etc);
- administration of the prison library and the collection of teaching material; and
- deputising for the director of the institution or departmental directors.[6]

The prisoners are offered a variety of educational opportunities, therefore, depending on the functions particular to the institution in question, including primary education – reading, writing, arithmetic and German as a foreign language; courses aimed at obtaining secondary school qualifications or professional qualifications; and lessons of recreational interest or responding to personal choice. Computer courses are just as common as language courses. Courses range from literature, political education, painting, handicraft and music, to yoga, meditation, chess or social training.

School and professional examinations must be taken under the supervision of the authorised public examination boards. At the Correspondence University of Hagen, prisoners may attend and be examined in suitable courses of study, in which prisoners are guaranteed accompanied or temporary leave from their institution for any examinations they may need to take.

Since it is often the case that there are only a few full-time teachers in the penal institutions, those courses taken with a view to obtaining qualifications, which tend to be more demanding in terms of personnel, are offered in certain special institutions. Prisoners in one particular region who are interested in the course are brought together in that institution for the period of the course.

Conditions for personnel

The Federal German penal institution teachers are either civil servants or employees of the State, as are their counterparts in the public schools. They have received educational pedagogical training as well as specialised education from a university or college. Most teaching staff come either to teach middle-level school qualifications (10 school years) or to teach professional qualifications. Often the penal institutions co-operate with the local Open University, while recreational courses are often offered by teachers in a voluntary capacity or by those working part-time. The costs for these courses are partly paid by Prisoners' Help Groups.

Since there are no specific training or university courses for teachers in the penal system in the Federal Republic of Germany, such teachers are insufficiently prepared for these duties at the beginning of their employment in penal institutions. Teachers from special schools for youths with learning and behavioural problems and others with the relevant specialised qualifications, are only seldom to be found in employment in penal institutions. Out of more than 400 penal institution teachers, only 30 have such special educational training (Cornel, 1994: 345). But even these teachers lack important knowledge in the areas of criminology, criminal law, administration of justice theory and organisation theory.

Courses offered in penal institutions should be motivating; the participants should have fun while learning; there should be an atmosphere created which both stimulates and encourages trust, and the participants should be given the opportunity to experience a feeling of achievement. Thus it is necessary to have qualified educationalists with the right experience. So, many penal system educationalists must gain the necessary specialised knowledge, partly from the areas of pedagogy for the educationally handicapped and for the disturbed, and partially from the science of rehabilitation as well as related complementary scientific areas. They must do this either in the form of courses for the further education of teachers, or otherwise autodidactically. Often the 'jumping-in-at-the-deep-end' effect of working practice, or the 'learning by doing' effect, together with a committed searching for help and advice from the well-informed will lead to success. Such well-informed further educational and supportive courses are offered by the 'Federal Association of Teachers in the Penal System eV', which was founded in 1958. This has at present 240 penal system teachers in its ranks, and at an annual national conference it set itself the goals of providing specialised further education in problem areas related to working practice and education in the penal system; and providing seminars for beginners and basic support to those in the profession.

Further educational seminars on specialised areas and management topics

– in which the teachers may participate – are also offered by the education authorities and administrative authorities of each State, as well as on a national scale. For the most part, the extent to which such professional training seminars are taken advantage of depends on the initiative of the teachers themselves. The supervision of educational work in the penal system usually rests in the hands of jurists or high-level administrative officials, who find it difficult to assess the efficiency of educational intervention, intentions, goals, methods and qualifications.

Penal education in practice

What is the present situation of educational work in practice in the penal institutions of Federal Germany? The lack of the most elementary education is an expensive stigma in prison. Favours such as the writing or reading of a letter often have to be repaid in some form (eg tobacco or coffee). Comradely acts of unselfishness are rare. What is more, time spent inside a cell can become very long, when the accustomed set of tools for filling your free time is not available. Prison life can feel very claustrophobic, when you can neither read nor write. Where words and the ability to argue are lacking, violence and auto-aggression can occur very quickly. As a result of a misjudgement of their actual situation, however, many prisoners often avoid admitting to their shortcomings and requesting the necessary lessons, because they are afraid of losing their personal dignity and reputation. Often, therefore, they miss out for much longer than is necessary on the chance of receiving support and further education from the educational staff of the penal institution. In many cases, such prisoners are first brought to the attention of the teachers in the institution only by chance, when somebody drops a hint, thus enabling them to offer teaching and support to the prisoners. Then, only when teaching begins, is the full extent of the shortcomings revealed. The progress which the course participants can make and the results they can achieve depend on the variety of differences in ability, learning tempo and individual hindrances to learning. The basic conditions of the lessons vary from institution to institution, and depend on the commitment and qualifications of the teaching staff, as well as on the teaching and learning materials which are available and the size of the groups.

As regards the number of participants, the teacher in penal institutions has the advantage that she/he can work with extremely small groups, and sometimes even give one-to-one coaching. Of course, this depends upon the educational measures being recognised as being indispensable, as is, for example, the case with primary education. As a rule, there are never more than a handful of participants in the literacy courses, the most basic level of the elementary education programme. Most other courses are taught in groups of between 10 and 15 participants.

The fact that the prisoners are available round the clock even makes it possible for the hour-by-hour elementary teaching to grow into an integrated course. In this way courses can include not only lessons in reading, writing, arithmetic, political education and social training, but can also go so far as to include a basic education in natural science and technology, aesthetics and the fine arts, or domestic science and the skilled crafts. In this area, the penal institutional education system has a large amount of leeway in how it organises and conceives its courses. This is the case so long as the system succeeds in portraying the courses as meeting the needs of the prisoners, and as being necessary for their reintegration into society and helpful in producing a favourable prognosis for the quota of subsequent offenders.

The prisoners usually readily accept educational opportunities, since the lessons are for the most part more varied than work, and are paid just the same: on average a 10 DM training allowance per day. In many cases, participants are transferred to school-level or professional qualification courses after successfully completing their elementary courses, provided that the length of their prison sentence suffices. Should this not be the case, the teachers make endeavours to find educational establishments, for example, in co-operation with the employment office – outside the institution – where the prisoner can continue, or begin, his further education after release. The fact that such attempts do not always succeed to the extent which one would wish is symptomatic of the problems and difficulties in the whole area of resocialisation. Its success depends on many social, economic, but also quite personal, reasons and causes – for example, widespread addiction to alcohol and hard drugs.

As a rule, the established educationalists of a prison determine the educational needs of their institution with the help of their teaching experience, their personal educational advice to the prisoners and the informal conversations with the remaining colleagues, including the social workers and psychologists. It is on the basis of this analysis that the programme of teaching and training courses is planned and then, according to the personnel and financial possibilities, often with the co-operation of such public institutions as the Open University. A penal institution is particularly fortunate if committed people or institutions from outside offer to support the educational work through teaching or by holding other events.

One project which should be mentioned here is the exemplary Readers' Club Project set up in 1990 by the author Marie-Thérèse Schins and the College for Educational Sociology in Hamburg, represented by Professor Peter Budweg, which has worked together with students in the Hahnîfersand reform school, situated on an island in the Elbe. The initiators of this project wanted to 'build a bridge of letters between them there on the inside and us here on the outside' (Schins *et al*, 1994: 11). Here, texts, books, stories and magazines were read in a relaxed atmosphere once a week with juvenile offenders who had little or no reading abilities. A writing workshop also came into being, because the participants themselves started wanting to relate things about their own lives and talk about their feelings. On top of training in reading and writing, they also developed a feeling for the importance of the written word, learned to be proud of things they had written, experienced feelings of success and thus the motivation to continue. Soon the themes being discussed, read and written about became more and more varied: childhood; education; family; love; drugs; music; friendship; adventure; and many others. This creative approach towards basic education points us in the right direction. Basic education must be 'meaningful and must change your life', it must develop perspectives for the future, help the prisoners to discover abilities and help them to come to terms with life (Schins *et al*, 1994: 161).

Similar projects, experiments and committed concepts of education can also be found in other places. They show us that educationalists working in penal administration and penal institutions in the Federal Republic of Germany are also aware of the significance of basic and elementary education for prisoners and that they have a legal right to education.

Peter Sutton from the UNESCO Institute for Education hits the nail on the head when he refers to the fact that 'criminal justice cannot solve all the social problems of the individual and of society'; but training and education received during the prison sentence can provide new chances for prisoners to 'organise their lives so that they can feel partially satisfied' after being released. This integrates prisoners back into society and reduces the danger of them committing a subsequent offence. Sutton formulates his thoughts on the importance of receiving education while in prison in the following impressive way:

> *In exactly the same way as each cell in our body repeatedly regenerates itself during one lifetime, so can a man's life take a completely new direction, no matter how old (Schins et al, 1994: 165).*

Education in the penal system contributes to this effect.

Perspectives

With the information depicted above, there can remain no doubt that the law-makers in the Federal Republic of Germany now recognise the significance of schooling and professional training, or in the wider sense of personality formation, as being important for the reintegration of prisoners into society.

However, the translation of this guiding principle into practice more often than not meets with difficulties. The necessary extent of educational opportunities is a subject for debate, with each person having their own opinion, depending on their position and perspective. For committed educationalists and educational sociologists, the need has only been met when prisoners who are willing to be educated have been able, successfully, to find their way out of their social fringe groups into satisfying working and living conditions, without delinquency.

The perception of the general public, however – encouraged by frequent negative reporting in the media, by generalisations and by the over emphasis of spectacular individual cases in the press – is that costly subsidies are out of place for imprisoned delinquents. Here, people are much less prepared to look at the matter from a different angle, or to take a close look at the fates of those concerned and the chances they may have in life. Often one hears people talking of the 'futility of love'. The perception that victims of crime do not receive the same level of attention reduces the readiness of people to recognise the right of prisoners to education and personal development. However, the consciousness of caring for the victims and the possibilities of reaching a settlement between perpetrator and victim have grown noticeably in legal, criminological and penal educational circles in the last five years, although with a more realistic assessment of what is achievable.

For politicians and the state, fiscal and economic thinking and planning usually take precedence over willingness to take efficient education into the penal system by introducing the necessary measures and personnel. This is understandable in view of the current difficult economic situation, but from the special educational perspective it is still unsatisfactory. One thing has cost enormous amounts of money since reunification, and that is the reconstruction of the administration in the so-called 'five new States' of the Federal Republic of Germany. Penal institutions still need to undergo thorough building redevelopment, in order to bring them up to date with modern security standards. Some of the personnel still need to be trained according to the basis of West German Penal System Regulations and Concepts. In this respect, there is still an accumulated need to be met in many areas of the New States before we can claim to have reached sufficiently modern standards to enable us to call it a quality penal system.

But even in the Old Federal States – again because of the situation described – many desires of the penal educationalists for more effective personnel and financial opportunities will have to remain unfulfilled for the time being. From the expert's point of view, this can only be regrettable, since it is often the enthusiasm for new models and the taking of initiatives in the educational field which leads to developments and to qualitative improvements. It would be necessary, for example, to design and test structured educational concepts and forms of organisation specific to penal education, which integrate the training and further education of the prisoners in closed and open imprisonment with the probation assistance and aftercare of released prisoners. Also, in the Federal Republic of Germany, there is a dearth of up-to-date and extrapolated research into the theory of and scientific back-up for penal education, because personnel in the institutions are often not given sufficient room for manoeuvre for such 'sidelines'.[7] But these are important in order to evaluate and extrapolate the present concepts. Only in this way could the necessary educational goals, content and needs of the work be analysed on a satisfactory scale and then newly defined on the basis of the latest changes.

At the present time, the penal system teachers are having to deal with the challenges of an increasingly high percentage of foreigners – in some institutions up to 50 per cent – as well as an increase in violence and organised gang crime. New main emphases and different methods are called for in educational work, if the staff are to be able to react to these current factors in the prison population in an adequate way, as described in the goals of penal education. A considerable percentage of the available teaching staff will have to be moved from the traditional orientation towards the obtaining of school-level and professional qualifications as well as content- and process-oriented and specialised learning goals to more general goals, which are more oriented towards behaviour and evaluation (Pendon, 1994: 205). Modularly structured educational and training programmes would have to be expanded and extended in order to gain the flexibility needed to cope with the changing needs of prisoners. Here, the enormously improved opportunities of the new electronic, or rather new media, educational technology could be helpful in making teaching more individual and in getting the students more interested in education and motivating them to take advantage of the more attractive and more comprehensive offers of 'open learning'.

Thus, educational work in the penal institutions of the Federal Republic of Germany continues to provide us with tasks which must be successfully managed. In the same way, however, it also provides us with opportunities and chances, on the one hand to improve educational provision for prisoners as well as their skills for coming to terms with life, and on the other hand to organise the penal system in an up-to-date and modern way. Whether this progress can be realised will depend not only on the commitment of the penal educationalists alone but also, for the most part, on politicians' understanding of the importance of education and its delivery with appropriate aid and support.

References

Baumann, U. (1996) 'Registrierungskarrieren von Strafentlassenen', Zeitschrift für Strafvollzug und Straffälligenhilfe, No 2/96, pp 67–78.

Bund der Strafvollzugsbediensteten Deutschlands e V (ed) (1995) Handbuch für den Strafvollzug, Berlin/Bonn.

Bundesarbeitsgemeinschaft der Lehrer im Justizvollzug e V (ed) (1995) Lehrerinnen und Lehrer im Justizvollzug. Beschreibung eines pädagogischen Arbeitsfeldes, Straubing.

Busch, M. (1990) 'Erziehung als Strafe', Zeitschrift für Strafvollzug und Straffälligenhilfe, No 3/90, pp 133–139.

Cornel, H (1992) Die soziale Situation Haftentlassener. Daten zur Sozialplanung far die Straffälligenhilfe in Berlin, Berlin.

Cornel, H (1994) 'Zur Situation, Funktion und Perspektive des Schulunterrichts im Justizvollzug heute', Zeitschrift für Strafvollzug und Straffälligenhilfe, No 6/94, pp 344–348.

Council of Europe (1990) Education in Prison. Recommendation No R (89) 12, adopted by the Committee of Ministers of the Council of Europe on 13 October 1989 and explanatory memorandum, Strasbourg

Deimling, G (1980) Erziehung und Bildung im Freiheitsentzug. Gesammelte Aufsätze zur Straffälligenpädagogik, Frankfurt/M.

Deimling, G/ Lenzen, H. (1974) Straffälligenpädagogik und Delinquenzprophylaxe, Neuwied/Berlin.

Eberle, H J (1980) Lernen im Justizvollzug. Voraussetzungen und Ansätze einer Justizvollzugspädagogik und ihrer Didaktik, Frankfurt/M.

Eberle, H J (1982) 'Didaktische Grundprobleme der Bildungsarbeit im Justizvollzug', Zeitschrift für Strafvollzug und Straffälligenhilfe, no.2/28, pp 101 ff.

Eisenhardt, T (1978) Strafvollzug, Stuttgart.

Heine, W (1866) Die Besserung als Strafzweck und das Aufsichtsperonal der Strafanstalten. Ein Beitrag zur Gefängnislehre, Leipzig.

Heuer, G (1977) Zur Diskrepanz zwischen Anspruch und Wirklichkeit der Strafanstalten, dargestellt am Fall Karl-Heinz G, Rheinstetten.

Hoffmeyer, C. (1979) Grundrechte im Strafvollzug. Verfassungsrecht als kriminalpolitischer Beitrag zur Reform des Strafvollzugs, Heidelberg.

Kaiser, G/ Kerner, H J/ Schöch, H (1991) Strafvollzug. Ein Studienbuch 4. Auflage, Heidelberg.

Kette, G (1991) Eine sozialpsychologische Analyse, Göttingen, pp 6ff.

Krebs, A (1974) 'Es begann mit Religionsunterricht', in Deimling, G/ Lenzen, H (eds) Straffälligenpädagogik und Delinquenzprophylaxe, Neuwied/Berlin.

Leuss, H (1903) Aus dem Zuchthause, Berlin

Mehner, H (1992) 'Aspekte zur Entwicklung des Straf- und Untersuchungshaftvollzuges in der ehemaligen sowjetischen Besatzungszone (SBZ) sowie in den Anfangsjahren der DDR', Zeitschrift für Strafvollzug und Straffälligenpädagogik, No 2/92, pp 91 ff.

Ministerium der Justiz Rheinland-Pfalz (1986) Grundsätze der pädagogischen Fachabteilung der Justizvollzugs- und Jugenstraf- anstalten. Rundschreiben des Ministeriums der Justiz vom 10.12.1985, Mainz.

Ortner, H (1988) Gefängnis. Eine Einführung in seine Innenwelt, Wienheim/Basel.

Pendon, M. (1994) 'Lernziele im Vollzug', Zeitschrift für Strafvollzug und Straffälligenhilfe, No 4/94, pp 204–205.

Quensel, S (1981) 'Zum Pädagogischen Ansatz im Justizvollzug', Zeitschrift für Strafvollzug und Straffälligenhilfe, No5/81, pp 278 ff.

Schatz, G (1989) 'Chancen und Grenzen Pädagogischen Handeln im Strafvollzug', Zeitschrift für Strafvollzug und Straffälligenhilfe, No 1/89, pp 14 ff.

Schins, M-Th/ Wagner, S/ Budweg, P. (1994) Vergitterte Jugend. Innenansichten aus einem Jugendknast, Recklinghausen.

See, W (1983) Nun büßt. mal schön. Szenen aus dem Strafvollzug, Frankfurt/M.

Strube, W (1931) Untersuchungsgefängnis Berlin-Moabit, Berlin.

Vogel, K-D. (1992) 'Zum Stand der Alphabetisierung im Justizvollzug der Bundesrepublik Deutschland', Zeitschrift für Strafvollzug und Straffälligenhilfe, No 2/29, pp 112–116.

Wagnitz, H B (1791) Historische Nachrichten und Bemerkungen über die merkwürdigsten Zuchthäuser in Deutschland, vol 1, Halle.

Walter, M (1991) Strafvollzug. Lehrbuch, Stuttgart.

Notes

1   For instance, The Ministry of Justice in the State of North Rhine Westphalia has been considering since the beginning of 1995 reducing the number of full-time teachers in the penal system by up to 25 per cent in the name of rationalisation. This comes after an investigation based on considerations of profitability was carried out in the organisation (the so-called KIENBAUM – report). But they are doing this without even carrying out an adequate analysis of the assignment of duties and results of the work of the teachers in the penal system (see press report of The Ministry of Justice in NRW (Publ); Investigation of Organisation; NRW Penal System under Scrutiny from an Economic Perspective, press release from 17 January 1995.

2   For more comprehensive information on this subject see, eg: Kaiser *et al* (1991), 48f and 65 and also Mehner (1992) pp 91.

3   According to: Act on the Execution of Prison Sentence and the Regulations Concerning Improvement and Security – Penal Act of the Federal Republic of Germany (St Vollz G) from 16 March 1976.

4   According to the 'Directory of Penal Institutions within the Federal Republic of Germany'.

5   The statistical details are reported from the publication of the Ministry of Justice of Lower Saxony, Hanover 1994.

6   A detailed portrayal of the job outline and thus also of the educational work done by the Federal German penal educationalists is offered in the brochure: 'Teachers within the Penal Institution: Description of an Educational Field of Work' published by the Federal Association of Teachers in the Penal System eV.

7   The present approaches are for the most part somewhat dated, compare: Deimling/Lenzen (1974), Deimling (1980), Elberle (1980), Quensel (1981), Elberle (1982), Schatz (1989), Busch (1990).

Chapter Seven

Filling the gap: education in Latvian prisons

Maris Mednis, Chief Specialist, Social Rehabilitation Section, Latvian Prison Administration

An estimate of the achievements in prison education of the three Baltic States shows Latvia to be behind Estonia and Lithuania. In Latvia, prison education is the problem of the day and there are crucial issues to be resolved, both by implementing advice from other European institutions and by the Latvian government's will not to undervalue penal policy in a context of fiscal and business policy.

Relevant statistical information

Although statistical evidence always has drawbacks the following figures give some idea of the context and size of the problem, and indicate some current trends.

General information

The total number of prisoners in Latvia is high. On 1 January 1997 it was 10,316 including 4,081 remanded in custody – the population being about 2.6 million and constantly decreasing.[1]

The number of recorded crimes between 1991 and 1996 were: 1991–42,000; 1992–62,000; 1993–53,000; 1994–41,000; 1995–39,000; 1996 38,205 (Vilks, 1997: 6).

The average length of prison sentence for convicts in 1996 was 54 months for men and 36 months for women.

The number of convicted prisoners is decreasing, whilst the number of untried prisoners is rapidly increasing. The convergence of the numbers of sentenced and non-sentenced prisoners is the result of recent changes in the legal procedure extending the process of appeal and changes in sentence.

Educational levels

Enquiries about the educational level and intentions of convicts (sentenced prisoners) produced the following figures. On 25 February 1994 about 45 per cent of convicts had secondary education, 30 per cent had incomplete basic education, and nine convicts were illiterates. About three per cent wanted to

Table 7.1 Number of prisoners in Latvia

Date	Prison population			Number of prisoners per 100,000 inhabitants
	sentenced	untried	in total	
1 July 1994	7,240	2,312	9,552	367
1 July 1996	6,654	3,735	10,389	400
1 September 1996	6,526	3,588	10,114	389
1 January 1997	6,056	4,081	10,137	390

gain (that is, enter or complete) basic education. Three per cent of convicts wanted to gain secondary education. About two per cent wanted to improve their professional skills.

One of the conclusions from the inquiry was the inadequacy of information available to prisoners about education. The prisoners were unaware of current developments and main trends in the labour market. This was no surprise – even people outside prison without such stigma and lack of liberty are short of complete information. Even representatives from the Ministry of Education and Science, close to planning future development, seemed to evade such questions when posed.

The habit of constant decision-making has not yet pervaded Latvian society. Particular attention must be given to prisoners in this regard. A high proportion of prisoners are severely disadvantaged people suffering from negligible educational experience and a shortage of necessary information. Therefore, there is a need not only to educate them but also to teach them to want to learn.

The 'average literacy' of the prison population is low. It is difficult at the moment to evaluate the most essential cognitive and basic skills as the outcomes of the formal educational system are not providing the most appropriate criteria.

We also have to take into account an increase in the number of adolescents truanting from schools in society outside prison. There was no information about this five years ago, but, partly as a response to new-found freedoms, in 1997 about 15,000 youngsters were not attending school (Avotins, 1997: 2). But during the last three years the natural growth of population was minus 47,000 (Baltins, 1997: 2), with migration to and from Latvia also negative – emigration exceeded immigration.

Nevertheless, it is still considered to be better to avoid the need to educate people in prisons by means of trying to educate them in society.

Table 7.2 Sentenced prisoners and their educational levels

	25 February 1994	24 May 1996	Increase or decrease
Number of prisoners	6,678	7,463	+ 11.76%
Educational level (classes completed)			
without education and illiterates (less than 1 yr)	9	48	+ 433.33%
not completed initial education (1–4 yrs)	51	61	+ 19.61%
initial education (4 yrs)	38	233	+ 573.16%
not completed basic education (4–9 yrs)	1,375	1,999	+ 45.38%
basic education (9 yrs)	909	744	− 18.15%
not completed secondary education (9–12 yrs)	868	611	− 29.61%
secondary (general, special, technical) education (12 yrs)	3,392	3,711	+ 9.40%
higher education (including not completed)	36	56	+ 5.56%

The historical context of prison education in Latvia

During the Soviet period in Latvia – from 1940 till the early nineties – Soviet Law was in force in all spheres of life including prison and education systems. Depending on age and educational and professional background, both work and education – or either work or education – for prisoners were compulsory. There was a system in force of general education until 1990 and professional education until 1991 for prisoners both sentenced and non-sentenced. The Prison Administration – serving prisons called Youth Labour Colonies for juveniles, or Correctional Labour Colonies for adults, apart from the Riga Central remand prison and Daugavpils top security prison – provided schools with rooms, necessary equipment and materials. Educational authorities, both central and local, were the employers and administrators of teachers.

In addition to general and professional education, the third opportunity in education was on-the-job training totally carried out by the employer – (that is, the production services of prisons.

During the years 1990–1991 a major part of this system was abandoned by the Ministry of Education and the Department of Prisons of the Ministry of Interior, due to lack of finances to maintain the schools.

Table 7.3 Some statistics about inmates in prisons (1 July 1996) [2]

Prison	Untried (including juveniles where applicable)	Convicts (including juveniles where applicable)	Employment of sentenced prisoners (per cent)	Distinguishing features of education in the prison
Brasas	15	591	25	general education
Central	2,375 (142)	136	100	–
Cèsu (male juvenile)	17 (17)	163 (163)	5	wide range – general, vocational, cultural; professional librarian
Daugavpils	561 (39)	567	20	professional librarian
Grivas	–	1,123	15	professional physical educators – with Norwegian assistance
Iguciema (female)	181 (3)	268 (3)	45	wide range – general, vocational, cultural
Jèkabpils	–	387	20	vocational training
Jelgavas	–	817	20	–
Liepâjas	313 (17)	–	–	–
Matisa	118	361	25	self-education
Olaines (open, male/female)	–	44	100	–
Pârlielupes	–	435	15	vocational training
Skirotavas	–	1,025	10	–
Vecumnieku (open, male/female)	–	39	100	–
Valmieras	155	698	10	–

Table 7.4 Participants of the state formal education system in prisons[3]

Prison	General education establishment	Vocational training establishment	Pupils	Teachers
Brasas	branch	–	120	6
Cèsu	school	centre	240	20
Iguciema	branch	branch	65	9
Jèkabpils	–	school	75	4
Pârlielupes	–	school	124	9
		Total:	**624**	**48**

The aims and purposes of the system

The system of legal regulations dealing with prison education still lacks careful thought and simply reflects the imperfections and typical inertia of the law. Public opinion in general is hostile to prisons and prisoners. The public can still think only of prisons as 'schools for criminals'.

At the same time many volunteers make significant contributions in time and other ways. Amongst them Christians serving in prisons provide spiritual and religious development and support, which are close to the very purpose of education, though these volunteers do not claim to be educators.

Education in prisons is still envisaged as a kind of luxury and appendix to security regime and rules. In fact our penal policy can afford little else than the struggle for survival. Inhabitants of Latvia are comparatively poor, especially those engaged in prison and education services. The same applies to prisoners and ex-prisoners who are deprived, not only of liberty, but also of many things of prime necessity.

Recommendations in the Lakes/Rostad report

The Latvian prison system in general, and educational issues in particular, have been scrutinised by several independent bodies. One of the most significant was when the Council of Europe appointed Gordon H Lakes, former Deputy Director General of the Prison Service of England and Wales and (the now late) Mr Helge Rostad, a former Justice of the Supreme Court of Norway, to provide advice and guidance on how the prison system of Latvia might be brought into conformity with European Standards. They visited Latvian prisons in August 1994. An assessment was made of developments in the service and some valuable recommendations made.

The main recommendations relating to prison education are listed in Table 7.5.

Table 7.5 The Lakes/Rostad Report recommendations about prison education in Latvia and action taken in some prisons since the visit

Recommendation	Result
Paragraph 27.23 – *It is recommended:* 'that more extensive programmes of organised games and sports be developed in all prisons' (Lakes/Rostad Report, 1994: 113) 'that unused workshops or other buildings be taken into use as sports halls and activity centres' (Lakes/Rostad Report, 1994: 113)	There are programmes of organised games and sports in all the prisons, developed to a certain extent. Alas, professional physical educators either full- or part-time – are only in Iguciema, Grìvas, Cèsu Prisons. It is done in Grìvas, Valmieras, Pârlielupes, Jèkabpils, Matìsa, Brasas Prisons.
Paragraph 27.24 – *It is recommended:* 'that efforts be made to provide the necessary facilities and to recruit suitably qualified volunteers to enable prisoners to participate in educational activities of an academic or recreational nature. (See EPR Rules 77 to 81)' (Lakes/Rostad Report, 1994: 113–114)	Just a few more prisons and volunteers. Again Iguciema, Cèsu, Brasas Prisons should be mentioned.
Paragraph 27.25 – *It is recommended:* 'that the library facilities be improved by increasing the number and variety of books, newspapers and periodicals, and that where space permits, a reading/study room be provided' (Lakes/Rostad Report, 1994: 114)	Library in Brasas Prison was reconstructed – enlarged by 20 sq metres where presently 12,500 books are kept. An enlarged and comfortable room (65 sq. metres) allocated for religious ministers and reading/studies/lessons. Iguciema Prison received assistance from the Soros foundation enabling the subscription to newspapers and journals.
'that library stocks be changed periodically. (See EPR Rule 82)' (Lakes/Rostad Report, 1994: 114)	The books are received almost exclusively as gifts from private persons, public and religious organisations. Content and quality varies.

Current structures and management: legislative and structural framework

The existing legislative framework concerning the system of prisons and imprisonment was mainly inherited from the Soviet period and based on the

USSR Criminal Code,[4] the Criminal Process Code and Correctional Code – each was subsequently amended a number of times. These Codes and their subordinate legislation have continued to apply to the Latvian Prison system since independence. In 1995 the Codes were extensively amended by an Act of Parliament.

In particular, the Correctional Code was amended and renamed as the Execution of Punishment Code. The main reason for these amendments was gradually to move the Latvian system of the execution of punishment towards a Western European system, which was seen to have significant advantages. The principal distinction between the Soviet 'labour camp' approach and the 'prison' approach is the prisoner's ability to earn privileges, or the administration's prerogative to remove privileges. This enables prisoners to move to greater independence. The principal differences are depicted in Table 7. 6.

Table 7. 6. The principal differences between the previous 'correctional' and the present 'execution of punishment' approach to prisons in Latvia

Characteristics	Correctional labour colony	Prison
Living area	Mostly dormitories	Cellular confinement
Movement of prisoners in living area	Free 24 hours per day as a general rule	Limited to secluded areas, prohibited from 2200 to 0700 hours
Prison sub–culture	Influential	More under control
Privileges as incentives to good behaviour through regime differentiation	Less	More
Influence of the prison administration on the amount of privileges (due to the progressive system)	Less significant	More significant

Main regulations

Today we have inherited basic regulations concerning work and education in prisons from the Soviet period, but with one essential difference – work and education for prisoners should be compulsory. Unfortunately, the prison system in Latvia cannot afford to involve all prisoners in these activities.

Diplomas or Certificates for graduates from schools in prisons never reveal that the graduate is from prison.

Penal rules

The Latvian Execution of Punishment Code regulates how and where sentences of imprisonment must be served. Articles 62–67 are devoted to the education of convicts – Execution of Punishment Code, 1995: Articles 62–67 – and unfortunately resemble the structure and the imperfections of classification inherited from the Soviet period regulations. The law provides access to education only for: adolescents requiring general secondary education; persons who do not have basic education; and professional education for those who have not acquired specialised and on-the-job training – to improve the skills and to obtain the new speciality needed for the purposes of the prison institution. Even in these cases access to education is not always possible.

Educational rules

According to the Education Law – first enacted on 19 June 1991 and subsequently amended by Parliament – the united, continuous educational system which is established and constantly improved in the Republic of Latvia comprises:

1) upbringing before school
2) upbringing and education outside school
3) basic education
4) general secondary education; professional education and vocational training
5) special secondary education
6) higher education
7) improvement and change of qualification as well as self-education

(Education Law, 1991: Article 6).

Main supplementary rules

Some basic rights of the prisoner are described in the so-called Constitutional Law of the Republic of Latvia, *The Rights and Duties of Individual and Citizen* (in fact there is no Act about human rights or prior juridical force equal to Constitution 'Satversme', the second part of the Constitution of Latvia being still under preparation and not yet adopted) which was adopted by Parliament on 10 December 1991. Article 19 emphasises that 'a prisoner should not be deprived of the rights to . . . education' (Constitutional Law, 1991: Article 19).

Intentions and comments

However, the 'educational menu' in Latvia is not so developed and the range of educational needs and informational demands are comparatively narrow. The attention paid by the state to some important fields, for example, adult education, does not match their urgency.

Now the new legislation (Criminal, Criminal Procedure, Execution of Punishment – and Education Law) has been under preparation and subjected to extensive consultation for some time.

The adoption of a new Education Law will be possible when the 'state – local government – private person' relationship is established and local government reform becomes clarified by goverment decision.

Educational system

The present general practice of education in prisons in Latvia is unfortunately limited to general education as class subjects and vocational education. Both were almost exclusively carried out by teachers employed by the Ministry of Education and Science directly – in the case of professional education – or via local governments, until the latest developments, for general education. But in Cèsu Juvenile Prison both general and professional educators are becoming employed by the prison administration and ranking as prison staff. Other spheres of education – creative and cultural activities; physical education and sports; social education and library facilities – attract a non-professional approach, but this applies in few prisons and success depends on the competence and diligence of prison staff.

Prison system

The management and administration of the Latvian prison system is the responsibility of the Latvian Prison Administration, under the leadership of a Director General who is directly accountable to the Minister of Interior Affairs of the Republic of Latvia. The prison system in Latvia is subordinated to the Ministry of the Interior. The transfer to the Ministry of Justice has been discussed and initiated a number of times but constantly suspended. However, it is hoped that this is just a matter of time since a new intention to transfer on 1 January 1998 is depicted in a recent Cabinet Statement.

Characteristics of prisons

Description of inmates and their access to, and demands for, education to some extent vary in any particular prison. One prison is for juvenile delinquents (Cèsu); one – female (Iguciema); in some long-stay, mostly adult, convicts; in some first offenders, in remand prisons non-sentenced persons are in the overwhelming majority.

The access of prisoners to education facilities varies from prison to prison too. The best relevant opportunities are in juvenile and female prisons, but these comprise a low percentage of the total prison population. The main problems, however, centre on Riga Central Remand Prison where prisoners are not directly subject to the penal system but to the court, prosecutor, and investigating institutions. In such an ambiguous situation, no one has direct responsibility for their education. There are about 150 juvenile offenders in Riga Central Prison. Though not sentenced for imprisonment and not being found guilty and considered to have almost the same rights and opportunities as those being outside prison, nevertheless they lack any educational opportunities.

On the contrary, sentenced convicts are more mobile and their choice is wider. For example, convicts in Matìsa Prison – situated in Riga – are comparatively better educated. They themselves, individually or in groups, study foreign languages and business management. There are language courses – for example, English and German – in Jelgavas Prison and similar opportunities in other prisons.

Spheres of education in prisons

The possibility of gaining general secondary education is offered in Cèsu Juvenile Prison, where inmates can attend a secondary school fully under the auspices of the prison administration.

In Brasas and Iguciema Prisons there are centres of studies and personal tuition in evening courses at branches of local general education evening schools. Teachers are employed by local educational authorities, whilst the prisons provide rooms and materials. There was also such a branch in Jelgavas Prison in the 1995/1996 school-year with four teachers and 15 students attending classes. Early in 1996, however, the local government refused to employ the teachers and explained that there was no reason to educate prisoners who are reluctant to attend classes and who were not over-zealous. But the teachers were not professionals in adult education either.

Vocational training

Vocational training as part of the formal state professional education system of professional schools is provided in Pârlielupes Prison, Iguciemas Prison and Jèkabpils Prison. Cèsu Juvenile Prison runs a Vocational Training Centre of its own, as a minor variation from the usual pattern.

The vocational training of prisoners consists of training in painting; welding; repair or assembly of electrical and electronic equipment; and operating and maintaining heating equipment. Teachers are employed by central educational authorities (except in Cèsu), and the prison administrations are responsible for rooms and materials.

On-the-job training

On-the-job training for the needs of prison domestic services is offered in almost every prison, but these cover only a limited range of occupations – heating, electricity services – and serve only the number of trainees currently needed to maintain the system.

Libraries

Libraries outside prison come under the Ministry of Culture and librarians can receive their training there at least through the local branches. Books in the stocks of prison libraries were mostly out-of-date but now new ones are received through donations from public libraries, private persons, and publishing houses.

There are only two professional librarians, working in Cèsu Juvenile and Daugavpils Prisons respectively. Both of them are employed by the prison administrations. The prison librarians do not have the educational background appropriate to librarians, do not receive in-service training and can improve their skills only by educating themselves and establishing contacts with their colleagues and acquaintances.

In all the other prisons convicts are employed as librarians, but prison libraries are little more than book stores.

Physical education

Professional physical educators work in Grìvas and Cèsu Prisons. In Iguciema prison volunteers help a great deal and prison staff participate.

Art and culture

Art and cultural education are at their strongest in Iguciema and Cèsu Prisons. In almost every prison there are handicraft industry workshops where the inmates can make something – mostly woodwork – and then exhibit and sell their articles. In almost every prison there are recreational facilities containing halls where the inmates can play music, sing, discuss, and so on.

Religious work

The Latvian prison service considers religious work as one of the essential forms of education. It helps the prisoner to become acquainted with a valuable and acceptable way of life when assistance from the state system is still negligible and insufficient, and it is seen as reducing recidivism. Religious education was, and still is, carried out by volunteers. But, from 1996, a chaplaincy service under the auspices of the Prison Administration has been established.

In all of the prisons regular work of Christian religious creeds and parishes has been maintained since 1989. At least once a week representatives of Roman Catholic, Baptist, and Adventist Churches meet their parishioners, and a more active representation of the traditional Orthodox, Lutheran churches is now developing. The Baptist Parishes, Pentecost and Adventist Churches are the most active. Thirty-five Christians – chaplains, clergymen, ministers – constantly work in 13 prisons (Smirnovs, Mednis 1994: 6).

Their work consists of individual conversations with prisoners, including visits to cells; Bible, Gospel and religious literature lessons; public worship and prayers; spiritual concerts; and assistance to ex-prisoners and their families.

Particulars of curriculum, staff and other issues in prisons

This brief description of activities in some prisons indicates a variety of the issues involved.

Cèsu Juvenile Prison

General basic and secondary education here is accessible in the secondary school under the auspices of the Prison Administration. About 170 pupils are attending every school year. The two study languages are Latvian and Russian. There are 15 teachers having 20 years' length of service on average.

A so-called 'evening shift programme' is provided which involves some small variations from the standard curriculum. The main subjects are Maths, Literature, Grammar, History – with an introduction to Social and Political Sciences, English, German, Physics, and Chemistry. Teachers of Physics and Chemistry also act as laboratory assistants. There is no Physical Education in the curriculum of such a school. Nevertheless juveniles can participate in winter and summer sports and games, on a daily basis. One of the prison officers is directly responsible for the sports programme.

The main obstacle to the fulfilment of the syllabus is the uneven level of educational backgrounds and abilities of pupils, because the formal educational system has no flexibility. At present the number of secondary school pupils is in decline and that of basic school pupils is increasing.

Teachers have regular in-service training courses with payment being made for some of these.

Vocational training

There are facilities for vocational training. In the summer/autumn of 1996 a Government decision transferred nine vocational school teachers from the Ministry of Education and Science to the Ministry of Interior. They were re-titled as inspectors, their duties increased and their advantages diminished – payment; working hours; length of vacation; and disciplinary matters. So far, only five of the teachers have decided to become employees of the Ministry of Interior. The vocational school was subsequently re-organised to a Vocational Training Centre with a total of 14 job positions. Now 70 students are divided into six groups – three locksmith, one production (mainly woodwork), one painting, one turning. The recruitment of a juvenile to any of these groups must correspond to his unit and he is not entitled to move to any other vocational training group on his own initiative.

One of the advantages is that the vocational school can cater for a wider variety of educational backgrounds. To join the state school, a certain level of education – nine classes – is needed. This is not required to join the Centre. There are considered to be improvements arising from the new schedule –

more inmates can educate themselves and get the necessary skills in a timetable more geared to their needs.

The main disadvantages are felt by the teachers who lost part of their salaries, privileges and vacations; and those who decided to join the Ministry of Interior service lost their trade union protection.

Other facilities

In addition to the formal educational system, groups of juveniles trained in needlework and handicraft go in for sewing, picture frame making – four times per week; drawing – five times per week; music – twice a week; under the guidance of professional educators. Representatives from various state, public, and religious organisations visit juveniles and give lectures and concerts.

Iguciema Prison

The general secondary education establishment is affiliated to an evening-shifts school outside prison. There are four teachers and about 40 students, including convicted girls and untried prisoners.

Vocational training

The vocational training establishment is also affiliated to one of the local vocational schools. Five teachers work with about 25 students. The main occupation is sewing.

Other facilities

In addition to the formal programme a variety of activities takes place thanks to the initiative of the prison staff. In 1995 there were 31 and in 1996 76 prisoners, who passed exams and received Latvian language certificates. Language classes are provided with financial assistance from the Soros foundation, Latvia. English language classes are organised also by the Deputy Director of Iguciema Prison. Both English and Latvian are taught twice a week. Women are engaged in cultural activities; needlework; religious; medical and hygiene; physical activities; and mother-care education. A lot of assistance, for example in English and needlework courses, comes from the wives of the staff of the United Kingdom Embassy.

Brasas Prison

There is a general secondary education establishment affiliated to an evening-shifts school outside prison with six teachers and about 120 students per school year. Materials and resources are almost exclusively, as elsewhere, provided by the system inherited from the 'previous ages'.

Jēkabpils Prison

There is a vocational training school with four teachers and 75 students. The occupations taught are electricians; stokers; sewers; and turners. In addition, some inmates are engaged in handicraft workshops producing souvenirs and furniture articles.

Pârlielupes Prison

There is a vocational training school with nine teachers and 124 students. Occupations taught are electricians; locksmiths; welders; and electronics assembly workers. Facilities for general education were provided, but it proved impossible to start the programme because of the lack of financial support for teachers.

Grivas Prison

Grivas Prison has received aid from Norway, including training equipment and clothing for physical education and training. Games and competitions take place with inmates, sometimes with both inmates and staff participating. During 1996, 28 new open-air exercise grounds (27–40 sq m) with static sports apparatus were provided. Three open-air sport grounds – one of them for TB patients – are in place and indoor sport facilities (area 700 sq m) with all the necessary equipment: sauna and pool; wardrobe; showers; and rest-room are provided. Every day, at least 100 inmates from cells take part in sporting activities. Two professional physical educators – still lacking complete academic background and special training – are employed.

Paintings by prisoner-artists decorate the prison interior.

Current issues and problems

One of the paramount issues is the lack of professional educators – different from just teachers – in prisons. Especially when one considers the wide range of various forms of illiteracy amongst adults and adolescents which is constantly increasing in Latvian society and which is reflected in the prison population.

At the same time the responsibilities and duties of the prison staff are immense. Prison officers who permanently work with, and are directly responsible for, some prisoners – this position may be translated as 'head of inmate activities' or 'head of unit' – may be 'mother; father; executor; adviser; teacher; friend' to several hundred prisoners simultaneously. Their list of duties includes education; social work; psychology; in addition to regime management; security; supply; and domestic care.

Self-education

Self-education, though not prohibited by law is in fact accessible only on a limited basis. For example, one of the teachers proposed using English language correspondence courses. There were about 60 prisoners ready to join these courses and resources were made available for this activity. Despite the view that correspondence education is considered to be of lower quality than classroom teaching and that the drop-out rate could be higher, it was believed that introducing correspondence courses would at least ensure some level of activity.

Such an educational possibility (that is, by correspondence), as well as extra mail in this case, were not proscribed in the Law. But nevertheless there were, and still are, obstacles. Correspondence for prisoners is allowed and of unlimited frequency, but is subject to censorship. According to the Internal Regulations letters are not allowed when they are written in a foreign language without an obvious reason (Regulations, 1995: Article 137.-5). At present, no censors working in prisons understand any foreign language and as security services are afraid of any criminal contacts being established by means of letters in a foreign language the issue is still pending.

Higher education

Another problem concerns higher education. On the one hand this is an educational right prisoners are entitled to; on the other hand this right has to be put into practice via a procedure impossible for most prisoners. In Latvia higher educational establishments are autonomous to a certain degree and according to their rules, even if attendance at lectures is not obligatory, the physical presence of a student is required for all examinations including entrance examinations. At the present time, the Law does not allow prison leave for educational reasons. Prison leave is of a limited duration and strictly regulated according to reasons and procedure and categories of entitled prisoners (Execution of Punishment Code, 1995: Articles 50–5,50–6).

Extramural teaching and a distance learning approach are comparatively new to Latvia and just taking the first steps. Not enough attention is being paid to it, or to adult education, current library facilities, or the teaching of basic cognitive skills.

Latvian language

Another current problem is that of the Latvian language. On 1 September 1995, the national composition of the prison population was surveyed by the Department of Prisons. It transpired that representatives of 29 nationalities[5] are serving their sentences in the prisons of Latvia. The largest national groups of convicts are Latvians, comprising 47 per cent – in general society about 54 per cent – and Russians, comprising 40 per cent of the total number of inmates. Other nationalities include the following: 2–3 per cent Byelorussians, Ukrainians, Lithuanians; 1.5–2 per cent Poles and Gypsies; 0.4 per cent Russian Federation nationalities; 0.1–0.2 per cent Azerbaijanis, Georgians, Armenians, Moldavians, Jews and Germans; 0.01–0.1 per cent Estonians, Uzbeks, Tadjiks, Romanians, Slovaks, Iranians and Vietnamese. All the Latvians know Russian well enough to communicate, as for a long time Russian was the only language in use in the prison system – both by inmates and staff. Now the majority of this 53 per cent non-Latvian – sometimes called 'Russian-speaking' but in reality being rather 'non-Latvian speaking' – part of the population needs to be taught Latvian. The prison system is not responsive to developments in society.

Staffing and staff development

Teachers working in prisons receive 30 per cent more pay than all other teachers. But the number of teachers working in prisons diminished last year. Four teachers worked as general educators in Jelgavas Prison, but left as local educational authorities were short of money to pay them.

There will be no obvious improvement in this situation in the near future. On 27 December 1997 Article 57 of the Education Law was amended by Parliament (Education Law, 1991: Article 57) and a set of subsequent Regulations is being adopted by Government. Now only state educational establishments are to be financed from the state budget. All those employed in the local educational establishments will receive their salaries and any extra remuneration only from the budgets of local governments. The financing of local educational establishments is going to be the direct responsibility of local governments, and in some cases deals between some of them using 'Local Governments Finance Equilibration Fund' can be concluded. This system of payment is just being introduced and has not yet been tried out. Whilst the status of prisoners is still uncertain it is unlikely to be put into force.

Improvement of qualifications

The improvement of professional skills and qualifications for teachers is organised by their employers. But the Ministry of the Interior and individual prisons cannot provide the training for those who are employed by prison administrations. They can rely only upon the goodwill of the educational authorities. And there the dilemma appears – the Ministry of Education does not take into account education in prisons when providing improved opportunities for teachers' development. Whilst the prisons are interested in education, they lack the necessary finances and knowledge to develop staff.

Recent development

The Social Rehabilitation Section of the Latvian Prison Administration is still trying to introduce current ideas about prison education into Latvia. We deal with education in prisons, trying to facilitate some educational activities carried out by prison staff. The aim is to develop an appropriate system of education in prisons which conforms to European standards and, to that end, to co-operate with all the organisations concerned. Alas, our co-operation with the Ministry of Education and Science is far from meeting our hopes and, one supposes, the demands of prisoners. The main reason for this failure we consider to be the incoherence of, and flux within, the system. The Ministry of Education is experiencing greater change than the Prison Administration. The Educational Law was adopted in 1991. The new law has been in the process of being prepared for a long time. However, the proposed amendments received were three times longer than the draft itself. The system of financing schools has recently changed and will be the full responsibility of local governments with resources yet to be identified.

In such a situation we cannot fully develop the 'import model' in Latvia. Some of the draft regulations proposed with a view to establishing the prison education system in Latvia were based on the 'internal' model.

The main responsibility currently falls upon the prison administrations some of which, for example Iguciema Prison, have achieved a great deal.

Latvian adult education association

We have started to co-operate with the non-governmental Latvian Adult Education Association and are looking forward to a breakthrough for prison education in the near future. We are grateful to the Latvian Adult Education Association (LAEA) for their interest in these problems and for following up the view that 'the education of prisoners must in its philosophy, methods and content be brought as close as possible to the best adult education in the society outside' (Education in Prison, 1990: 8). In Latvia, adult education both inside and outside prison are to be improved.

During 1997 a seminar about adult education in prisons in Latvia was organised by the LAEA with experts from The European Prison Education Association (EPEA), British Council and 'Soros foundation – Latvia', and the Latvian Prison Administration for participants from Latvia. Any kind of assistance or interest from more experienced and successful colleagues helps us a lot. We hope the co-operation will continue. We are looking forward to bringing our prison education into line with European standards, experience and expectations.

Notes

[1] All the data about prisons and prisoners when the source is not specified are obtained from the regular accounts and random inquiries in Latvian Prison Administration Headquarters. The total number of the population of Latvia is approximated. Figures are average except when specifics are given

[2] All the untried prisoners are unemployed. Their on-the-job training comprises only that needed for heating, woodcutting, laundering, etc, and is not mentioned due to the comparative insignificance in average numbers involved (approximately five inmates or a small number filling job positions in every prison) and because of the similar situation in each prison.

[3] The numbers are average. For Césu and Iguciema Prisons figures are added. So the number of pupils in each, and the total number of pupils involved differ.

[4] In the references from legislative sources, the titles of and quotations from acts, laws, rules, and regulations may suffer from the lack of authorised translation and the dissimilar application of judicial terms in English and Latvian Law.

[5] In Latvia it is common knowledge that the term 'nationality' is not equal to 'citizenship' but means 'ethnic (language) origin'.

References

Literature

Avotins, V (1997) *'Katrs pats sava pretinieka kalèjs'* *('Everyone makes his own foe')*, *Neatkarìgâ*, No 23:2.

Baltins, G (1997) *'Vai sâcies ilgi gaidìtais tautsaimnieçìbas uzplaukums?'* *('Has the long awaited boom started?')*, Diena, No 36:2.

Council of Europe (1990) *Education in Prison*. Recommendation No R (89) 12 adopted by the Committee of Ministers of the Council of Europe on 13 October 1989 and Explanatory Memorandum, Strasbourg.

Council of Europe (1994) Report of a Council of Europe Co-operation Visit to Prisons etc in Latvia August 1994: The Lakes/Rostad Report, Strasbourg.

Vilks, A (ed) (1997) *'Kriminogènâs tendences 1996 gadâ un kriminâltiesiskâs sistèmas pilnveidoøana Latvijâ'* *('Criminal tendencies in 1996 and improvement of criminal law system in Latvia')*. Nacionâlâs noziedzìbas novèrøanas padomes Kriminoloâisko pètìjumu centrs, Rìga.

Smirnovs, I, Mednis, M (1994) *'Cietumnieku un no cietumiem atbrìvoto sociâlâs adaptâcijas un rehabilitâcijas procesa virzieni, saturs un dalìbnieki Latvijas Republikâ'* *('Direction, Content and Participants of the Social Adaptation and Rehabilitation of Convicts and Ex-convicts in Republic of Latvia')*, Rìga.

Legal regulations

Latvijas Republikas 1991 gada 19 junija Izglìtìbas likums, ('Education Law of the Republic of Latvia'), Zi_otâjs, 1991, No 31/32.

Latvijas Republikas 1991 gada 10 decembra Konstitucionâlais likums 'Cilvèka un tiesìbas un pienâkumi', ('Constitutional Law of the Republic of Latvia, 'The Rights and Duties of Human and Citizen'), Zi_otâjs, 1992, No 4/5.

Latvijas Sodu izpildes kodekss, ('Execution of Punishment Code of Latvia'), Riga, 1995.

Brìvibas at_emøanas iestâyu iekøèjâs kârtìbas noteikumi, stâjuøies spèkâ ar LR Iekølietu ministrijas 1995 gada 28 júnija pavèli Nr 245 ('Internal Regulations of the Institutions of Imprisonment (28 June 1995), enacted by the Ministry of Interior order No 245').

Chapter Eight

Prison education in the Netherlands – some issues

Robert Suvaal, Education Advisor, Ministry of Justice, The Hague, Netherlands

The National Agency of Correctional Institutions in the Netherlands consists of three different kinds of institutions: remand houses and prisons (18 years and older: about 11,500 persons in 40 state institutions); institutions for mentally disturbed delinquents (18 years and older: about 650 persons in three state and four private institutions); institutions for young offenders (under 18 years: about 1,050 persons in seven state and eight private institutions). So in September 1996 the Netherlands with a population of 15.5 million, had about 13,200 detainees, ie an incarceration rate of 85 per 100,000. Each sector had its own central management and policy. This chapter addresses the first, and biggest, sector only.

In the second half of the 1980s and the beginning of the 1990s, prison education in the Netherlands achieved a high level of service. In that period it was part of a prison service with a very good reputation in the international penal world. But in recent years there has been some deterioration. This chapter examines the origins of these positive and negative influences, referring to the influences abroad, both in society and in the prison service itself. The raw materials of the whole are my own learning experiences gained during a long career in the Dutch prison service. I begin by looking back briefly at the history of prison education in my country so that the reader can better understand the present situation.

The history of prison education in relation to developments in society and in the prison system

Halfway through the previous century there was already a kind of prison education in the penal institutions in the Netherlands, embedded within the regimes of that time. A quote in Eggink's book on prisons states: 'In 1836 it was prescribed that if useful, primary school education should be provided in the penal institutions' (Eggink, 1958). But this account starts at a much later stage.

After World War II the Dutch prison system soon became part of a positive development. An important role was played by the experiences of a number of Dutch people during the war in German, or Japanese detention. They had experienced the negative influences of detention themselves and thus had developed views about imprisonment; therefore, they had become expert advisors on questions of regimes. The 1970s and the first half of the 1980s were the peak in this positive development. The influence of the Director General of the Prison Service, Hans Tulkens, throughout most of that time was remarkable. Together with Englishman Ken Neale, his contribution to the penal philosophy of the Council of Europe was substantial. Moreover, the social and economic situation promoted development within the prison system for there was then a belief that the government could achieve the ideal society. There was a belief in the 'perfectibility' of society; the incarceration rate – the number of detainees per 100,000 inhabitants – was one of the world's lowest – approximately 35 – and the Netherlands supported a permissive criminal law culture (Brand-Koolen, 1987).

Prison education in the Netherlands in the 1970s was only well developed in two fields: physical education/sport; and libraries. This arose from the existence of national co-ordinators in these two fields; at the time there were no co-ordinators in the other fields. The 1970s were used to improve the quality and quantity of staff, programmes, accommodation and materials, but mainly in these two areas. Adult and further education remained marginal activities in prison. There were only a few teachers, mostly working full-time outside the prison, who would attend the penal institutions at night to provide individual instruction, sometimes using materials developed for children. A number of detainees participated in correspondence courses, although experts realised that this learning method was not the best for most detainees. Art education was still in its infancy too. There were various reasons for this situation. One was the lack of central direction, another was the fact that in the 1970s detainees were expected to work all day. And, of course, the major development of adult education outside the prison walls had only just started. The prison system itself was characterised by humane regimes concentrating upon the individual prisoner and the human rights of the individual detainee. For example, it was in this period that a formal right for all detainees to complain officially was developed and installed. These developments were all made possible by the belief that society was 'perfectible'; it was a placid and stable period in the penal field. Three detainees refusing to go to work one day constituted a riot.

The early 1980s both saw the development of adult and further education and art education. This chapter addresses mainly adult and further education, not so much because this discipline is the most important, but because the author's job focuses on these activities. At that time the social and economic situation was still favourable to positive developments in the prison system. In the mid-1980s the daily programme was changed. In the new system detainees were only expected to work half days. Half the prison population worked in the morning, the other half in the afternoon. The other half day was for the other regime activities – exercise; shopping; prison education; and so on. This radical change came about for organisational reasons. This new system provided some work in the workshops for nearly all the prisoners, whilst reducing the need for workshop accommodation and staff. The half day for work was not to be interrupted. This change to the new system was presented as an efficiency measure, although the ideas behind it were developed by Hans Tulkens from an ideological starting point! He believed that the relationship between prison officers and detainees was at the heart of the prison climate (Tulkens, 1991). In the half day system the prison officers would play an active part in the whole activities programme, including work. That was what was attempted, but in most of the institutions this experiment was not a success in the work sector. With some other activities it did succeed, especially in sport and creative activities. Training courses for these prison officers had preceded the experiments. But organisational problems have recently ended this situation. The irregular hours worked by the officers – shifts, night duty, leave and so on – made it impossible for them to attend activities on a consistent basis. A continuing problem was to plan the same officers regularly for 'their' activities due to night and weekend shifts and leave. It is a pity because I observed a real improvement in the relationship between prison officers and detainees.

This radical change in the daily programme was supported by an increase in the number of teachers and art consultants/teachers. This expansion was possible because of a small reduction in the number of prison officers and work staff. Another positive factor was that in those days a number of penal institutions were being built, expanded or renovated and classrooms and rooms for art education were incorporated in the plans.

In the 1970s and 1980s education both inside and outside Dutch prisons was called social-cultural work. Penal social-cultural work consisted of four disciplines, namely: adult and further education; library; physical education/ sport; and art education.

Between 1985 and 1994 prison education developed healthily towards the ideals of the Council of Europe report *Education in prison*, adopted by the Ministers of Justice of the Member States in 1989 (Committee of Experts, 1990). The report was published in 1990. Few failings were then evident in prison education in the Netherlands.

The state of affairs in prison education at the beginning of the 1990s

There follows a brief description of the state of affairs in 1992–1994. This description is more or less valid today, but in general it is a picture of deterioration, mostly by quantitative measures.

The participants

The detainees in the remand houses and prisons are 18 years and older. For many years our prison population has been very multicultural. It is made up of about 50 per cent Dutch with a Dutch cultural background; about 25 per cent are members of cultural minority groups – mainly people from Surinam; the Antilles; Morocco; and Turkey – and about 25 per cent are foreigners. More than 70 nationalities figure in our prison population. It is not rare for a sports team of 12 participants to include 12 nationalities. It follows that many languages are spoken in Dutch penal institutions. The prison libraries include reading materials in more than 35 languages. Normally English and Spanish are spoken in most of our institutions besides Dutch. Apart from this cultural and linguistic variety the prison population is, in terms of personal characteristics, not very different from that in most other countries. That is, most of the detainees are young – between 18 and about 35 years old – predominantly male – we have only about 450 female prisoners – and include a high percentage of drug addicts – about 60 per cent. They have on average a low level of education, training and work experience. Further, an increasing number of detainees need psychiatric care or supervision.

Participation

There is a legal right for all detainees to participate in adult or further education; physical education/sport; and work in the prison library. Unfortunately, there is no similar legal right to participate in art education. This is because it is the most recent development in prison education and has not yet been legally included with the other facilities. Such a right would be desirable, not only because of Dutch art history and culture, but also because of the functional and developmental opportunities presented by art education (Suvaal, 1995).

The quantitative levels of participation were satisfactory some years ago. The national averages can be estimated as follows: adult and further education (including vocational education), about 40 per cent of the detainees (mostly part-time participation, only a few full-time students); library, about 80 per cent; physical education and sport, about 70 per cent; art education (mostly creative activities), about 25 per cent, as a rough estimation. Participation is not compulsory. Compulsion would not work and it would be contrary to our adult education and penal philosophy.

In exceptional cases the governor can permit a detainee to study instead of work, with pay. For example, for university students it is becoming more common to establish 'contracts' between institutions and individual participants if they study in work time. This contract arrangement enables the student to take responsibility for himself or herself and promotes the role and status of prison education.

The concept of prison education and relationships with the outside world

Prison education in the Netherlands has adopted the adult education model, in terms of programmes, aims and respect for the client. The aims are educational, just as they are outside the prison walls, although efforts are made to focus on objectives useful for social reintegration – Dutch as a second language, vocational qualifications and so on.

The aim is to replicate the comparable social-cultural activities outside the walls, so relationships are developed at national, regional and local levels. Some educators are employed by the institutions but educators working both inside and outside the penal institutions are welcome. These contacts are necessary to avoid the isolation of prison education and fit well into the Netherlands pattern of voluntary prison employment with all its other advantages, especially in terms of acceptance and commitment.

A national curriculum and other documents provide a basis for mutual conformity between penal institutions; this is necessary for several reasons, but particularly because of the many transfers of students between institutions.

The place in the daily programme

Within the basic programme structure of half a day work and half a day for other activities, a detainee works either in the morning or in the afternoon. Work may not be interrupted in favour of other regime activities. The other part of the day is intended for social-cultural activities and attending to personal requirements, such as exercise, shopping and visitors. Detainees can use their 'free time' during evenings and weekends for recreational activities such as television, playing table tennis, cards or chess. In contrast to work, social-cultural activities may be interrupted for lawyers, visitors, doctor and other appointments. This is a big disadvantage for the continuity of educational activities. The detainees have only limited influence over these interruptions and this can lead to unfortunate competition between activities – for example, sport versus adult education – or a shortage of time for educational activities.

The prison education teams in institutions

All institutions have a social-cultural team – or prison education team – consisting of: a head of the team who is comparable to the education officer in United Kingdom and Ireland; teachers; librarians; instructors for physical education/sport; art teachers or art consultants. All members of this team have the same qualifications as are required outside the prison. The ratio is 1:27, ie a penal institution with 270 detainees has 10 full-time staff for prison education. Since the recent devolution – or decentralisation – in 1989–1990, the institutions can hire external educators.

More than 60 per cent of the teachers are women just as in the outside adult education colleges and a number of female instructors provide physical education/sport in penal institutions for male detainees. Mostly this works very well!

Unfortunately the number of prison officers actively engaged in prison education activities is decreasing quickly and is becoming a thing of the past.

Accommodation, methods and other resources

The available accommodation, methods and other materials are at a reasonably satisfactory level across all four disciplines. There is good sport accommodation, even a number of mini soccer fields with surfaces of artificial grass that can be used all year. There are well stocked libraries with a good system of support points for books in all the languages we need; sufficient and well equipped classrooms; most institutions have personal computers for prison education and software for computer-assisted learning and most of the institutions have good studios and workshops for creative activities.

The methods used are the same as outside the prison with the preferred teaching methods being student-oriented, ie his or her questions or learning needs are primary, with emphasis given to the active involvement of the student in problem solving. A large number of learner-active materials are used, and standardised teacher-support materials are available. The use of distance learning is limited because of reservations about its suitability for many detainees. At a higher level some detainees follow the high quality, modular courses of the Dutch Open University.

The institutions get a standard amount of money to utilise in accommodation and renew educational materials. The standard for materials in 1992/1994 was about 200 US dollars a year per detainee (= per cell in my country). But in the first half of the 1990s this resource began to lose its earmarked status as responsibility for the allocation of budgets was devolved to governors whose local decisions could erode the educational allocation.

Supervision, coordination and team development

There are three education advisors/co-ordinators employed centrally by the prison service: one for the prison libraries; one for art education; and one for adult education, further education and physical education/sport. These advisors/co-ordinators play an important role in the development of prison education policy; the supervision of the quality of prison education; the co-ordination of prison education; external and mutual co-ordination; and staff development. They work together with national working groups consisting of educators from the penal institutions and if necessary with external experts. The members of these working groups are regional representatives of the educators, chosen by these educators themselves. The national advisors/co-ordinators are the permanent chairpersons of these working groups. The main tasks of these working groups are: prison education policy development and advice to the central management; developing national curricula – always involving external expertise; planning and organising regional or national study meetings for the educators; setting up and maintaining a system of information experts for each curriculum area – for example, for Dutch as a second language; and editing and distributing national reports, bulletins and newsletters. There are two meetings a year for each group of educators, mostly regional meetings. Every two years there is a national conference for each discipline. These meetings are not only directed at the development of expertise, but are also meant to develop and maintain networks and mutual co-ordination and, last but not least, they are intended to support the morale of the educators and to provide them with fresh inspiration.

Developments post-1993 and future threats

As has already been indicated 1989/1990 saw the inception of another radical operation: a far-reaching devolution of tasks and responsibilities from the central level to that of the institutions. The motto of the operation was revealing: 'deconcentration, or else . . .' The main objective of this operation was to gain more control over the costs of the prison service. So the responsibility was delegated to governors because they spent most of the total budget and from that moment they were seen as managers of intergrated operations. The new management concept can be summarised as follows: a global national policy framework with more or less autonomous local managers with their own planning and control systems. The next step was logical and fashionable, making the prison service an independent agency – globally responsible for its activities and administration to the Minister of Justice but no longer part of the core ministry.

The 1990s are characterised by policies giving rise to reduction in public expenditure. The belief in the perfectibility of society fell away and this reinforced the financial policies. The first outcome of these structures was a number of suddenly occurring calamities: hostage situations and attempts to escape with help from outside, often with violence; of equal significance was the continued increase in the number of detainees. The public formed the opinion that 'if nothing works why go to such expense'. The demand for cheaper methods of detention increased. This call was of course taken up by politicians. Even leftish politicians became less and less progressive. Economising measures were promised to the parliament, affecting not only the prison service, but also general education, health care, social security, and so on. This is also the 'consultancy era', when the influence of external consultants and training advisors had a marked effect upon the prison service. Concepts such as: integral management; privatisation; planning and control; the client–provider model; total quality management; audits; measurement of output; and performance indicators came into play and a management ethos became the order of the day.

This whole trend was expressed for the prison system in the production of an official report called *Werkzame detentie* – translated: *Laborious detention*, but due to the translation some word play gets lost – which reflected current opinion (Ministry of Justice, 1995).

In summary this report recommended first, that detainees in remand centres and prisons should work nearly all day (the so called standard regime). Beyond this there would be only opportunities for activities described within legal rights. Second, only the detainees who could prove a motivation beyond legal rights activities would have the opportunity to participate in special programmes (treatment, education and training etc), the so-called 'plus regimes'. Third, there would be different regimes. Most detainees – about 75 per cent – would stay in the standard regime (26 hours' work net a week). For the rest of the detainees there were three kinds of 'plus regimes', namely: a regime for detainees who need psychiatric care; a regime for detainees who want treatment for their drug addiction; and a regime for detainees who want to participate in integral programmes directed at social reintegration – education, training, work training, guidance, but also attention for housing, health and relationships. This social integration regime is meant for only about five per cent of the detainees. Recently a so-called 'sober regime' was installed for detainees with a certain status – for example, remand prisoners and foreigners waiting for expulsion – who will stay only very briefly – maximum two months – in a penal institution. This regime is even stricter and simpler than the standard regime.

The consequences for prison education are obvious. There is a big threat to both the qualitative and the quantitative levels of activity. In a number of our institutions the combination of *Werkzame detentie* and the demand to cut budgets is leading to a slimming down of the size of the education team and the education programmes, especially in the 'sober regime' and the 'standard regime'. The legal right to participate in education is an insufficient basis to challenge these ideas. And this is having a particular effect upon the quantitive measure of activity. Existing levels have also diminished as a consequence of financial devolution, lump sum budgets and so on. European recommendations do not have a big impact in these circumstances. It is not that all governors wish to reduce their education programmes; a number have been protesting, some of them even in the press. The problem is that the reduction of their budgets forces them in this direction. As an integral manager of a penal institution with various disciplines and sometimes different interests they have to make difficult choices. A reduction of expenditure on security is not very easy; nor is it sensible for a governor to reduce expenses for work in the current climate. So prison education is one of the few options vulnerable to economies. One problem is that in many institutions there is not enough work for the detainees in the standard regime. In the near future that could work to the advantage of prison education. In many ways the problem is one of the image of prison education. Although the economy of Holland is improving, public opinion does support what prison education is trying to achieve. The only measure to be applied is that of recidivism, which is not the only valid instrument. But this view does not hold sway against the reality of public opinion. Terminology has been changed and social-cultural work is now called prison education, and attempts are made to clarify and publicise the utilitarian effects of prison education. But this is not an easy path and the education advisors realise that the threats are considerable, fearing that prison education will regress to where it was 25 years ago. Whilst all efforts are being made to rescue the service it is a strange feeling to work in a service that was recently called 'correctional' whilst the mission of the agency speaks only in terms of 'secure, effective and dignified custody' – 'reintegration' is not mentioned in this mission as it is included in the missions of the prison services of, for example, Canada and the United Kingdom.

A personal evaluation of 25 years of prison education in the Netherlands

After more than 25 years in this job – although since 1985, re-organisation has changed it every two or three years – I would like to add a personal assessment. As a 'lifer' – that is, 20 years in my country – I can look back over a long period of ups and downs.

My observations are mainly: broad social and economic trends inevitably influence developments and opportunities in the prison system. These trends come and go and act like a pendulum, swinging very slowly from control and security towards treatment, education and training; it is nearly impossible to resist these broad trends of control and security; in Holland we did well in terms of programme development and provision, networking, staff development, and so on, but we did not perform well enough in terms of evaluation (measurement of effects, output and outcomes), public relations and promotion. During a trough it is not sufficient to say that prison education is a good thing in its own right. The major problem for prison education is an international one: how to prove that what we do is useful and important?

I have come to the opinion that those of us concerned with and about prison education should address the following issues: sentence planning; integral (multidisciplinary) approaches; co-operation with other disciplines in the prison (work, social work, health); and working closely together with organisations outside the prison walls; experimental curriculum developments; individualised learning routes; selected combinations of different educational methods and intent (eg classroom education and drama); development of national standards for prison education; evaluation techniques and the developments of performance indicators (what works, how do we know and how can we measure this?) as part of a total quality management concept; good public relations and promotion (local, regional, national) focussed on outcomes.

References

Brand-Koolen, M J M (1987). *Studies on the Dutch prison system*. (Ed) Amstelveen.

Committee of experts (1990). *Education in prison*. Strasbourg: Council of Europe.

Eggink, J W (1958). *De geschiedenis van het Nederlandse gevangeniswezen*. Assen: van Gorcum & Comp. NV.

Ministry of Justice (1995). *Werkzame detentie*. Den Haag: Ministry of Justice.

Suvaal, R (1995). *A wide concept of prison education: luxury or necessity?* The Hague (paper for the EPEA conference in Blagdon, UK).

Tulkens, J J J (1991). 'Education in prison: is it about the trumpets or about Jericho?' In P Bedford, R Suvaal, W van Zon. *How high the walls*. (Report of the 3rd European conference on prison education). Enschede: SLO.

Chapter Nine

The education of convicted prisoners in the Polish penal system

Waldemar Strzalkowski, The Central Board of the Prison Service, Poland

The Polish penal system treats the education of convicted prisoners as one of the most important means of resocialisation – besides the exposure of a prisoner to discipline and order and to cultural and educational activities – attempting to achieve the principle aims of imprisonment, to counteract a relapse into crime. This is governed by the Order dated 19 April 1969 – the Executive Penal Code in Art 37, paragraph 2.

The need to provide prisoners with education arises from the following circumstances: about two per cent of condemned persons have not completed primary education before being arrested; about ten per cent of condemned persons have no vocational qualifications; about five per cent of prisoners require vocational requalification to increase their chances to find any job in their places of residence after release; about three per cent of prisoners apply to have their education and professional qualifications raised to secondary level. Polish researchers – amongst others, A Kobus and P Wierzbich in their book *Resocjalizacja wiezniow a powrotnosc doprzestepstwa (Resocialization of condemned persons and their relapse into crime)*, Warsaw 1967 – have shown that acquiring an appropriate general and vocational education in penitentiary units increases the ability of released prisoners to adapt to life in society, to find employment and thus counteracts a relapse into crime. Education establishes a set of values and beliefs and modifies the behaviour of prisoners, thus supporting individuals' resocialisation programmes and influencing their conduct after release. Also, filling in a prisoner's free time with educational activities reduces the onerousness of sentence and has an important therapeutic function.

Government guidelines concerning prison education

Rules concerning prisoners' education are in Art 54 of the Executive Penal Code and in paragraphs 51 to 57 of the Statutes on Execution of Imprisonment Sentence. A generalised outline of the rules is as follows: a convicted prisoner has a right to education at the schools which are provided in a penitentiary unit; a convicted prisoner has the right to apply for the approval of the Prison Director to learn outside the prison in an extension or extra-mural course, including studying at higher schools. Such approval may be granted only when security considerations do not make it impossible. A prisoner granted such approval has the right to educational leave and is subject to the same conditions and rewards as employees of socialised establishments; a prisoner who has not completed primary education or has not got any profession, who is under 50 and who has to serve a sentence of at least six months, and whose state of health allows it, has to attend educational classes in a primary or vocational school programme. The Prison Director may exempt a prisoner from this obligation if good reason is given. Education is provided in a prisoner's free time. In some cases the Prison Director may reduce the working hours of a prisoner who attends classes for up to six hours a week. Education is free: prisoners with no financial resources are provided with school books and resources without charge. A prisoner receives a certificate of completion of a school or professional course as he would outside, without any indication that he has received it during a prison sentence. A prisoner freed before the termination of a school year or completion of a course may take the final examinations in the prison; a prisoner freed before results appear receives a certificate that he attended such a school and a copy of his marks sheet is sent to the school where he is going to continue his course.

The education of prisoners in Poland is provided according to the Order controlling public education, dated 7 September 1991. It means that all educational regulations apply, with the exception of those affected directly by imprisonment: for example, the confidentiality of the business of a school council does not apply to schools attached to prisons where security may be affected; there are no schools councils involving pupils and parents at schools attached to prisons; there is no school or course board in prison schools; however, there are no prisoners' groups with similar functions. They have less authority and are controlled by a member of the prison staff.

Educational programmes provided at the schools attached to prisons are similar to those provided for that type of school in public education. Thus, students follow a common curriculum which allows the continuation of education at the same type of school and the possibility of progress into further and higher education.

Educational progress is the same as in public education for adults. Regulations concerning admissions, marking, promotion and issuing of certificates are the same for all public education.

Teachers in prison schools are civil employees and are required to have the qualifications demanded by educational regulations, subject to the Order dated 26 January 1982 (with subsequent amendments) of the Teacher Charter, which regulates the rights and duties of teachers, including questions concerning their remunerations – teachers in prison schools receive the same remuneration as the other Polish teachers according to their level of education and their working period. They also receive an allowance recognising the difficult working conditions, amounting to 50 per cent of a basic remuneration.

By virtue of the Order of the Council of Ministers dated 18 September 1992, defining types of schools and other educational institutions to be provided and supervised by ministers, and defining the duties and authority of those ministers – the Minister of Justice provides, maintains and supervises schools attached to prisons. Responsibility for the supervision of teaching of general subjects falls to the Education Curator's Offices, that is regional agents of the Ministry of Education. However, responsibility for the teaching of professional subjects, resocialising projects and compliance with educational law by prison schools, is exercised by those officers with appropriate educational qualifications employed in the Central Board of Penitentiaries (CZZK) according to the Order of the Minister of Justice dated 22 May 1990. This order deals with the supervision of the vocational schools in prisons and the Penitentiary Secondary Schools for Working People and defines responsibility for secondary schools. This responsibility involves assessing the effectiveness of schools in achieving ideal aims; achieving the appropriate level of teaching of various subjects; achieving the resocialisation aim of a prison sentence; and organisation complying with the educational regulations and the orders of the Ministry of Justice.

General inspections of prison schools are carried out by the educational inspectors of CZZK, together with the officers of the Education Curator's Office, who assess the level of didactical and resocialising activities, examine compliance with educational law and report on the level of activity in a school.

The organisation of teaching penitentiary units; the authority and scope of teachers' and school masters' duties; the regulation of collaboration between schools and the administrations of the penitentiary units; the management of establishments and the subsidiary farms employing prisoners; all fall under the Order of the Ministry of Justice No 47 dated 15 September 1983, on rules and procedure of teaching in prisons, which was signed in co-ordination with the then Ministry of Education and Upbringing, at present: Ministry of National Education.

However, the detailed procedure of the administration of prisons relating to the enrolment of prisoners for training and school tasks are set out in instructions (BP/ZP-861/91) issued by CZZK.

Some prisoners attend education voluntarily; others by virtue of an official order issued on grounds of the educational duty imposed on some prisoners according to the regulations of the Executive Penal Code.

Statistics showing the numbers of prisoners who attend education classes

The statistics of prisoners sent to education within the programme of primary schools – or the equivalent, primary vocational schools – show that about 75 per cent of prisoners apply for this activity on their own initiative. It also shows that about 25 per cent have no motive to learn and they are sent to education by virtue of an official order. It must be emphasised that the analysis carried out by the pedagogical supervision of CZZK in the year 1989–1990 has shown that about 32 per cent of prisoners who attended schools attached to prisons had failed to learn in primary or vocational schools. Those school failures often created defence mechanisms which caused a kind of depreciation of values, leading them astray. These prisoners are characterised by an aversion to school institution and learning. Their great fear is of further failure.

Practice has shown that the development of personal relationships between teachers and those students characterised by an aversion to learning can lead to a gradual raising of achievement. Appreciation of each pupil's intellectual efforts leads to cognitive developments resulting in a shift in values. Such pupils begin to believe in their own abilities and achieve positive didactic results. The switch from negative attitudes towards learning is a chance to complete education and acquire a profession. About 80 per cent of prisoners attend vocational schools on their own request and about 20 per cent attend compulsorily. However, prisoners apply for admission into secondary schools only on their own initiative.

Schools are provided in 30 prisons and in one remand – investigating – prison in Warsaw, they are organised into 23 school groups.

Generally, Polish schools are divided into: schools for young children (primary schools from the age of 7 to 15); schools for non-working youths (vocational and secondary schools from the age of 15 to 20); schools for adults (primary, vocational and secondary schools from the age of 18). Schools attached to prisons are schools for adults. Prisoners are classified thus; juvenile; adult first offenders, and recidivists, who are deemed to need individual methods of resocialisation.

First offenders may be detained in prisons for juveniles or recidivists, but must be in separate cells. The rule is that prisoners from various classifications cannot be kept in the same cell. Juveniles may mix with first offenders, first offenders may mix with recidivists for employment, training or cultural and educational activities; however, juveniles may not be sent to participate in these activities together with recidivists because of the possibility of detrimental influences.

Prisoners will attend an educational or training programme which accords with the aims of the prison and the group detained there.

Schools for juveniles with sections for adult first offenders are provided in eight prisons (including two working centres. Schools for adult first offenders with sections for juveniles or recidivists are provided in six prisons; however, schools for recidivists with sections for adult first offenders are provided in 16 prisons.

There is also a primary and vocational school for women in Penal

Institution No 1 in Grudziadz where convicted women are sent regardless of their classification group.

Grading prisoners within the education system

Prisoners are directed to education by penitentiary committees, that is joint bodies of the administrations of prisons. After prisoners are allocated to a prison, they are admitted by a prison committee which confirms the appropriateness of sending them to a particular unit. Prisoners are then enrolled on the educational programme, by checking their individual classification group, health, abilities to practice a profession, and ability to learn. Candidates are informed of the character of the unit; the conditions attached to education, what specialised training is available and what is involved; the duration of the resocialisation process; and what is expected of the individual, as a prisoner, employee and pupil. Then candidates are put into so-called 'school habitation sections'. The class teacher, together with a psychologist, prepares an individual programme of resocialisation which defines the tasks needed to adjust each prisoner's behaviour, and provides the individual with the necessary knowledge and skills which will make it possible to adapt to social and professional life after release. This programme describes the tasks which are to be performed by the prisoner, the teacher, the school and the working institution where the prisoner is employed. The resocialisation programme is negotiated with the prisoner who may make significant contributions to it. The programme is verified each six months, along with periodic assessment of the prisoner's progress.

Education is mandatory for each Polish citizen under 16. Primary school is the first stage of education and covers eight years (Classes 1–8). Former pupils of primary schools may apply for admission to elementary vocational schools or to general and vocational secondary schools. A former pupil of elementary vocational school has a certificate of qualification and may practice an acquired profession or get further education and vocational qualifications in a secondary school. The pupil may take up a job according to his or her vocational qualification of so-called 'medium technical centres' – ganger, machine setter, quality controller. However the former pupils of general and vocational secondary schools who have achieved a certificate of secondary education may apply for higher schools.

The following types of schools are attached to prisons.

- Primary schools, or equivalent vocational primary schools, provide programmes of 7th and 8th class of primary school in an annual cycle and prepare for a profession. After three years' practical experience a pupil may be examined for the status of qualified worker by the State Board of Examiners. Elementary vocational studies prepare for one of the following three professions: fitter, joiner, tailor.

- Elementary vocational schools with two-year courses prepare prisoners for one of the following professions – fitter, fitter-mechanic, welder, mason, concrete placer and steel fixer, farmer, tailor, purse maker, shoe maker, saddler, barber, bookbinder, printer, plastics processing machine operator, cook, joiner, joiner-upholsterer, RTV assembler, wire-man. Former pupils of these schools achieve the status of qualified worker.
- Vocational secondary schools have three-year courses for the former pupils of primary schools and two-year courses for the former pupils of elementary vocational schools. They are taught one of the following specialisations: mechanics, woodworking, printing, building, clothing, footwear and electronics. Pupils of the vocational secondary school do not acquire professional qualifications like pupils of elementary vocational schools. This type of school is intended to educate at secondary school level and generally instruct the pupils in the use of modern technology within broader fields of work.
- Technical secondary schools, with three-year courses – after completion of an elementary vocational school – train for one of the following three specialisations: machine construction, machining and general building. On completion, a pupil acquires a technical diploma in a defined specialisation and may take an examination for a certificate of secondary education. Primary and vocational primary schools are provided in 19 prisons, elementary vocational schools in 31 prisons, vocational secondary schools in four prisons.

Vocational training for prisoners

Besides training and educating prisoners in school situations, the Polish penal system provides other vocational training, described below.

Statistics for the last five school years have shown that about 15 per cent of all prisoners are provided with education in schools attached to prisons – including 20 per cent juveniles, 30 per cent adults condemned for the first time, and 50 per cent recidivists. This breaks down as follows:

- primary school or equivalent – about 700 pupils, that is two per cent of all prisoners, in the proportion of 50 per cent juveniles, 30 per cent adult first offenders, 20 per cent recidivists;
- elementary vocational schools – about 2,600 pupils, that is eight per cent of all prisoners, in the following proportion 20 per cent juveniles, 30 per cent adult first offenders, 50 per cent recidivists;
- vocational training – about 1,500 of participants, that is about three per cent of all prisoners, in the proportions of 45 per cent juveniles, 35 per cent adult first offenders, 20 per cent recidivists;
- secondary schools, that is, vocational secondary schools and technical

secondary schools – about 750 pupils, that is two per cent of all prisoners in the proportion of 5 per cent juveniles, 45 per cent adult first offenders and 50 per cent recidivists.

Education for juvenile offenders

The proportion of prisoners attending education in various types of schools according to their classification group is connected not only with their level of motivation for learning, but also with their length of sentence. Condemned juveniles acquire rights to apply for conditional release ahead of time after serving one-third of their sentence. Adult first offenders acquire the same rights after serving a half of their sentence and recidivists after serving two-thirds of their sentence. One must add that light sentences are passed on juveniles and heavy sentences are passed on recidivists.

It follows that juveniles who are given light sentences and who may apply for conditional release after serving a third of their sentences cannot complete a full two-year educational cycle at elementary vocational schools. Neither can they complete a two-year secondary education, or a three-year technical secondary education. So most juveniles participate in the shortest forms of training, that is in vocational courses lasting from 4 to 10 months.

The examination process for prisoners

During the years 1989–1994, 18,143 prisoners attended education at schools attached to prisons and 6,721 prisoners participated in training. This gives a total of 24,864. These figures break down across the various types of school as follows: primary schools – 3,311 persons – 1,728 former pupils; elementary vocational schools – 11,138 persons – 286 former pupils; vocational secondary schools – 2,578 persons – 554 former pupils; technical secondary schools – 1,126 persons – 120 former pupils. The examination for a certificate of secondary education was passed by 192 students of secondary schools. The State Board of Examiners examined in 12 schools attached to prisons.

During this five-year period the extension examinations within the programme of primary schools were passed by 91 prisoners; in elementary vocational schools 114 prisoners passed; and in vocational secondary schools, that is, vocational school and technical secondary school, 62 prisoners passed.

The State Board of Examiners also conducted 322 complementary examinations in special cases, for example, one prisoner had completed the 1st class of vocational school in a specialisation which is not taught in the system of schools attached to prisons and had to pass a complementary examination to attend the 2nd class – conferred 112 qualified worker titles, that is, examinations in professional training; examinations for students preparing to practise a profession after meeting practical experience requirements. They also conducted 201 examinations for the status of master in a profession. These examinations were passed by 193 prisoners.

Also during this period, 90 prisoners studied outside their prisons and with the approval of Directors of their prisons, including 16 at primary schools; 21 at elementary vocational schools; and 14 at secondary schools. Thirty-nine took up studies, among them 36 former pupils of schools attached to prisons.

Special educational needs

The penal system also provides education at 'special' primary schools for prisoners with learning difficulties who are often the patients of the therapeutic and educational sections in two particular prisons, Rawicz and Wronki.

Employment opportunities

However, when psychological diagnosis indicates that a prisoner can meet school requirements there are attempts to send such prisoners to elementary vocational schools, vocational courses, and there are even cases of sending such persons to secondary schools. This is done to give this type of prisoner the opportunity of employment. Although the outcome is often uncertain, it should be emphasised that 72 out of about 100 educationally backward prisoners who attempted various forms of education managed to complete their schools or courses. In fact one of them – a former pupil of a vocational secondary school – has passed an examination for a certificate of secondary education.

Summary of school statistics

A summary of the statistics covering these school years should emphasise that a total of 25,766 prisoners attended various forms of education and professional improvement in the system of schools attached to prisons. Also, 90 persons were given permission to study outside their prisons, 39 of whom have taken up studies.

About 70 per cent of prisoner students complete their course; the remaining 30 per cent are affected by various factors, such as orders of the courts and police which transfer prisoners or require their attendance as witnesses – about 10 per cent. In many cases, such prisoners are seen as being highly motivated and will continue their education post-sentence. Sometimes a deterioration of health makes it impossible to learn and practise a profession. Security measures – usually prisoners damaged by the prison subculture and resistant to penitentiary influence, and school failures – make up another about 10 per cent.

Organisation of schools attached to prisons

The organisation of schools attached to prisons is varied and ranges from four to 18 classes per semester. A total of 215 teachers are employed in such schools, 98 of them as full-time employees, and 117 as part-time employees. The average working life of a teacher is 19 years; 202 teachers are graduates with teacher training; 13 teachers have completed secondary pedagogical education – these are instructors in vocational courses.

The prison schools provide 198 classrooms for 4,100 pupils. Visual equipment and teaching aids vary, but every school has the minimum of equipment to cover their curriculum requirements. There are problems with the supply of equipment, but these are being solved gradually within the budgetary constraints of the penal system. Each school has a library where 'library lessons' take place; these develop skills of independent searching for information. Pupils have direct access to school libraries, may borrow any necessary book and use reference books in the library or in an organised reading room. There are also central libraries in each prison with library points in living areas for the use and recreation of all prisoners.

Librarians may provide readings through intercom systems installed in all prisons, or in organised meetings for prisoners. The penal service also organises readers' competitions, quizzes and local book fairs.

Range of facilities in prisons

Each prisoner has the opportunity to express her or his interests, needs and preferences, and may spend her or his free time using a wide but varied range of facilities offered in prison. These may include cultural and educational activities such as occasional meetings involving interesting people such as actors and politicians; concerts performed in the prison or outside; theatrical performances organised inside the units or in theatres outside; sporting activities and training (most prisons have professional equipment), table tennis, basketball, volleyball, football – are organised throughout the year on a regular basis in the prison area or, sometimes, competitions with sport teams take place outside. Programmes are broadcast through a central system, including popular and scientific programmes, quizzes, announcements, musical requests, and so on; TV programmes and video films – TV sets, tape recorders, videotape recorders, some belonging to prisoners, others to the prison, are available in most cells. Some units are equipped with satellite installation and prisoners who do not have access to receivers in their cells may use them in club rooms provided in each living area. There are interest clubs: music, film, discussion clubs, bridge clubs, drawing, poetry, computing, foreign languages and academic societies such as informatics, Polish language, mathematical, technical, natural history and so on. Each unit provides some free books and newspapers to prisoners.

Also provided are board games; outside visits for selected groups of prisoners and educational excursions to places of employment outside the prison, and museums in the case of students.

Besides cultural, educational and sporting activities convicted prisoners may also ask for religious assistance given by 233 prison chaplains who serve all prisons.

There are also groups of Alcoholics Anonymous in 60 prisons and Abstainers Clubs in seven prisons, where support is offered to alcohol-dependent prisoners. Withdrawal treatment is also provided in six prisons – RAS Warsaw; ZK Sluzewiec; ZK Kraków-Podgórze; RZK Wroclaw; ZK Barczewo; and ZK Nowy Wisnicz. Treatment in two of these prisons, RAS Warsaw and ZK Sluzewiec, is based on the ATLANTIS programme. The development of two further ATLANTIS programmes are planned in ZK No 1 in Grudziadz and in ZK in Ilawa. Some elements of the programme are provided in four other establishments; ZK Wronki; ZK Lubliniec; ZK Siedlce; and, ZK Chelm.

Significant attempts are made to develop co-operation between prison schools and students' families. Families are informed by mail when a student starts a course and are invited to co-operate. At the finish of each semester and school year, special parent-teacher meetings are organised. During these meetings families are informed about the educational and resocialisation progress of a student. Such meetings often result in the positive influence of families on students, who will encourage and motivate them to continue and complete their studies.

Achievements of the prison administration

The most important achievements of the prison administration are:

- consistently emphasising the importance of learning a system of values. This is indicated by an increasing interest in learning and the increasing proportion of prisoners applying for education on a voluntary basis. The proportion has increased from 40 per cent to 75 per cent at Primary School and Elementary Vocational School – with a corresponding reduction of the number of persons sent to education by virtue of an administrative decision;
- increasing the interest of condemned persons in increasing their professional and educational qualification in secondary schools. There has been an increase of secondary school expupils and the number of prisoners applying to take up studies has increased from 20 per cent to 55 per cent;
- formal teaching has become more closely integrated with resocialisation. This has resulted in an increase in the number of resocialisation programmes for individuals, with more formal didactic methods used as part of the

resocialisation process, and more effective co-operation between education and the penal authorities;

- improving the average grades of students from 3,00 in 1989 to 3,85 in 1994 and school attendance from 78 per cent to 92 per cent;
- the greater progress towards resocialisation of students than of other prisoners who do not receive education. This is manifested in the relatively faster progress of student prisoners, with more and higher rewards achieved and in the greater number of conditional releases ahead of time. The managers of employment establishments attached to prisons find that students are more interested in working, more independent and effective. Six per cent of prisoner students from second classes of elementary vocational and technical schools are employed in technical control at the level of gangers, quality control inspectors or masters.

In 1988, the inspector of penitentiary control of CZZK examined the educational level of all subjects at all schools attached to prisons. At the same time, the same tests were taken at schools for adults in three Educational Curators' Offices. The results showed that pupils from prison schools acquired higher marks by 0.1 per cent to 0.2 per cent in all subjects with the exception of maths where the average mark was lower by 0.2 per cent than in curators' schools. In 1989–1993 prison schools were subjected to selective testing; again, it was possible to record a consistent improvement in educational levels in these schools.

Some of these achievements have to be considered in the light of changes which took place in 1989 in Poland generally and in the Polish penal system. The political changes of that year led to changes in the penal code, the penal executive code and in the laws relating to temporary arrest and prison sentencing. The aim was to achieve consistency in sentencing policy. For example, before 1989, the penal administration strictly applied the rules requiring convicted prisoners to attend education and training. This often led to discipline problems and further punishment, such as solitary confinement. From 1990, CZZK has used only persuasion, thus improving motivation and relationships.

The two major problems of prison education in Poland are budgetary constraints – which mean that not all needs can be met; and the employment situation outside – which limits the number of prisoners who may be admitted to vocational schools. But the Central Board of Penitentiaries is working to relate prison education and training to labour market demands. It is important to get the basis right to anticipate improvements in the budget situation. Meanwhile, the Polish penal system is mindful of the recommendations of the Committee of Ministers of the Council of Europe Report on Prison Education, and attempts to work towards that ideal.

Table 9.1 Prisoners following education 1948–1993

Type of school or training	Persons in education	Number of former students
Vocational training courses	189,243	189,243
Education within the programme of a primary school	49,333	no data
Primary school	68,921	20,776
Elementary vocational school	125,995	35,232
Secondary school	14,368	3,620
Total	447,860	248,871

Table 9.2 Prisoners at Primary schools 1969–1994

School Year	Persons in education	Persons who have completed school
1969/70	4,031	1,783
1970/71–1979/80	45,595	19,273
1980/81–1989/90	16,777	8,284
1990/91–1993/94	2,518	1,436
Total	68,921	30,776

Table 9.3 Vocational training courses, 1962–1993

Year	Number of Courses	Number of former students
1962–1969	no data	50,577
1970–1979	2,952	70,852
1980–1989	2,741	63,240
1990–1993	218	4,574
Total	5,911	189,243

Table 9.4 Prisoners in secondary schools 1976/77 to 1993/94

School Year	Persons in education	Persons who have completed school
1976/77 to 1979/80	2,100	555
1980/81 to 1989/90	9,400	2,593
1990/91–1993/94	2,868	472
Total	14,368	3,620

Table 9.5 Training in primary schools 1948–1960

Year	Number of units providing education	Number of pupils
1948	47	1,861
1949	52	1,982
1950	63	2,066
1951	63	2,500
1952	68	3,775
1953	74	3,692
1954	63	3,345
1955	68	3,618
1956	63	2,871
1957	72	3,053
1958	85	5,709
1959	94	6,676
1960	100	8,785
Total	–	49,913

Table 9.6 Prisoners at elementary vocational schools, 1956/57 to 1993/94

School Year	Persons in education	Persons who have completed school
1956/57 to 1969/70	26,963	no data
1970/71–1979/80	47,919	18,738
1980/81–1989/90	42,430	14,322
1990/91–1993/94	8,683	2,172
Total	125,995	35,232

Chapter Ten

Developments in prison education in Sweden

Svenolov Svensson and Lis Somander, Swedish Prison and Probation Administration

Inmates/prisoners

Each year about 14,000 persons, of whom five per cent are women, are received into Swedish prisons. Their sentences vary from fourteen days to fourteen years, with a mean sentence length of 104 days. This means that the daily average prison population is about 4,500. During the 1990s an increasing number of life sentences have been imposed, although in practice this usually means 12–18 years in prison. Thus, in March 1990 there were 35 sentences to life imprisonment which, by 1995, had risen to 57. About 25 per cent of the daily prison population have a foreign nationality with almost one hundred different nationalities represented. Twenty-one per cent of the prison population are alcohol misusers; 21 per cent drug misusers; and a further 19 per cent misuse both alcohol and drugs. Approximately 10 per cent of the annual receptions into prison are in receipt of a disability or old-age pension.

Background

The Swedish criminal justice system comprises the police, the prosecution service, the courts, and the Prison and Probation Service. The system exists to control crime so as to create a lawful, just and secure society.

The Swedish Prison and Probation Service is required to work to reduce the likelihood of relapse into crime, without neglecting the need to protect society. The general framework for work with prison and probation clients is provided by relatively detailed legislation. Basic notions in the legislation are that there should be the least possible interference in the lives of offenders – hence community sanctions are preferable to custodial sanctions. Externally focused services – the community's various social and welfare services – are to be used as far as possible. Internal collaboration between the activities of the various branches of the Prison and Probation Service should be encouraged. Finally, all dealings with clients shall be based on a respect for their human worth and personal integrity. Education has always been emphasised as an important tool that makes, directly or indirectly, for the reintegration of offenders into society.

It is, therefore, both important and natural that prison and probation work is carried out in strict collaboration with other administrations and organisations such as, the social and health services, the labour market administration, various parts of the adult education system, and welfare and voluntary organisations.

The offenders who are the responsibility of the Prison and Probation Service have, in principle, the same rights as other citizens to the various services available in the community. For this reason it is important that work with prison inmates and clients on probation is integrated to the greatest possible extent with that of other bodies in the community. Underlying this approach is the idea that most offenders are people who function and react in most areas of life in ways that are not different from that of most citizens. This notion, usually called 'the normalisation principle', is a key concept in the management of Swedish prison and probation work, as it is in the other Scandinavian countries.

So far as education and vocational training are concerned, the normalisation principle has led to using the regular Labour Market Board training schemes for vocational training in the prisons. The services of the National Board of Education are used for other kinds of education. The period from 1975 to the beginning of the 1990s saw intensive co-operation between these administrations and the Prison and Probation Service, which led to an important enhancement of the educational programmes for prisoners. At that time all prison education was organised through municipal adult education schemes and was seen as a priority area in adult education. Several mutual projects resulted in guidelines for education in prison and an attempt to make education an important link to the outside world. During this period there were about 250 teachers involved in prison education. Some worked full-time in prison, but most of them divided their time between their regular municipal teaching and prison adult education.

In 1991 the Ministry of Education transferred equivalent funds to the Prison and Probation Service, which was then required to make use of the municipal adult schemes for prison education on a contract basis. This change occurred following a re-organisation of the National Board of Education and an emphasis on the decentralised financing of all public education. After 1994, however, public administrations must follow a new law on public purchasing. This law exists to guarantee that all public purchasing is done with a maximum of competition, to secure the 'right quality at the lowest price'. In consequence, a number of new organisations, both public and private, are involved in delivering educational services to the prisons. To date, fresh blood and high ambitions have had positive effects, but a loss of continuity may eventually emerge as a negative outcome. It is, however, too early to have a definite opinion on this matter. But one thing is certain – the prison administration must give a more clear and concrete expression to the aims of prison education and must become more competent at evaluating its outcomes.

Educational objectives

The Prison Treatment Act, Section 10, states:

> *Prisoners shall be provided with suitable work. Such work shall, as far as possible, further their prospects of adjusting to working life after release. A prisoner in need of education, vocational training, psychiatric or other special form of treatment shall be provided with an opportunity to receive such treatment during working hours if this can be arranged having regard to the length of the stay at the prison and the prisoner's personal capacities.*

This provision means that the prisoners' needs shall be the basis for educational programmes. Most inmates have uncompleted or only partially completed school as a common background. They also often lack real work experience and are drug-misusers. In planning individual treatment, the background has to be taken into account in order that the staff, together with the inmate, create a programme of individual activities/treatment during imprisonment, but also to serve as a basis for post-release preparation. Everything in the programme should aim at promoting personal growth and offer opportunities to adjust in society. The individual programme can include attending special personal change programmes – drug- or crime-related – working part-time in a workshop; and/or participating in prison education or vocational training. Inmates are obliged to take part in activities eight hours a day, five days a week, with exceptions sometimes made for pensioners. This requirement is not only an obligation for the inmate: it also obliges prison managers to provide full-time planned occupation for all inmates.

So far as education is concerned, special endeavours have been made to help inmates with basic difficulties in reading, writing and arithmetic. The general experience is that this group – whether composed of offenders or not – is not greatly interested in taking part in educational programmes. It is, therefore, an important task to try to involve them in prison educational programmes. Non-compulsory methods have been used and so far have met with some success. Considerable individual progress has often been observed together with a change of attitudes towards education and a sense of higher self-esteem. In addition to counteracting the well-known negative effects of imprisonment, such changes can be valuable after release.

Organisation

The organisation of prison education in Sweden is fairly decentralised. In each of the seven regions there is a co-ordinator responsible for prison education. Each prison has its own prison education officer or an officer with responsibility for all activities/programmes. The educational programmes are mainly – with vocational education as an exception – financed by the Prison and Probation Service and purchased, on contracts lasting from one to three years, from different public or private educational agencies. No teachers are directly employed by the Prison and Probation Service. Vocational training in the form of Labour Market Training is financed by the respective County Labour Boards. Each vocational course is run jointly through collaboration between the prison or regional administration and the Labour Market Board. One person in the central prison administration has, amongst other tasks, the responsibility for co-ordinating educational policy and guiding principles.

Prison education programmes

Many inmates lack the basic skills of reading, writing and arithmetic. In a recent study of the daily prison population made in March 1996, just over one third of the inmates considered that they had such difficulties. The most severe difficulty was experienced with arithmetic. In addition, inmates also often lack work experience and the social skills necessary for normal functioning in society.

In many spheres of activity, the community today makes stricter demands for an adequate education and training. In consequence, various kinds of occupational training in prison have been increased and production-oriented work has been reduced. In the 1950s, 'occupation' in prison meant, almost exclusively, industrial work. This has been gradually modified so as to include: studying at the prison; social skills training; assessment of work capacity; occupational rehabilitation; employment; and work and study release programmes. Currently, in most of Sweden's 75 prisons there are opportunities to undertake a variety of studies. The aim of treatment planning is to provide access as far as possible to the same educational opportunities as those available to ordinary citizens. In addition to study opportunities with varied content at most prisons, vocational training is organised interweaving theoretical and practical work. Education is mostly undertaken as basic adult education corresponding to middle and higher levels of elementary school education. Certain prisons provide study opportunities at grammar or secondary school level and, to some extent, even post-grammar school studies. Vocational training is undertaken in: mechanical engineering; industrial wood products; sheet-metalwork; welding; and, electrical engineering. Short vocational courses are arranged at several prisons. The central administration undertakes educational planning in collaboration with the National Board of Education and the Labour Market Board, as well as with regional and local authorities.

It is a political requirement that crime prevention work amongst prisoners should be intensified. This means that programmes must be devised and used that seek to prevent relapse into crime or substance abuse, by motivating prisoners to address their offending behaviour. In particular, such programmes must offer preventive help to inmates with an alcohol or drug problem and to those who have committed sexual or violent offences. Young prisoners and women prisoners need programmes which are especially oriented to their needs and characteristics.

For drunken drivers there are three different programmes at a number of prisons – the 12 steps AA programme; the Dynamic Cognitive Behaviour Modification Programme; and the Wisdom for Drunken Drivers Programme. Sexual offenders go through a special programme at some 10 different prisons.

The extent of prison education

Of all the sentenced prisoners received into prison during the period 1 July 1995 to 30 June 1996, approximately 6,500 undertook some form of study. This represents 46 per cent of the total number of receptions. The largest proportion of inmates who were studying were in elementary education. The following statistics give some idea how, and to what extent, prison education is used by inmates. Since some prisoners took part in more than one activity, the total number participating is greater than 6,500. Percentages have been calculated against the total number participating, ie 7,872.

Table 10.1 Use of prison education

Nature of activity	Number	Proportion (%)
Elementary education	4,284	54
Adult secondary education	443	6
Specific vocational training	852	11
Labour Market Board Training	700	9
Other education or training	1,593	20
Total	7,872	100

During the last financial year, prisoners were in education or special personal change programmes for 25 per cent of the time available for obligatory occupation. A current objective for the 1997 financial year is that this proportion shall be increased to 36 per cent of the time available for obligatory occupation. Qualitatively speaking, the ambition is to provide suitable education to every prisoner in need of education. But this ambition is limited by the fact that a high proportion of sentenced prisoners have extremely short sentences – 44 per cent of them are sentenced to two months' imprisonment or less.

Educational development

That the Prison and Probation Service shall work to ensure that the time in prison is used for activities designed to prevent relapse into further crime has achieved clear political expression. Currently, therefore, intensive efforts are being made to develop a range of personal change programmes, focused, in particular, on offenders with drug and alcohol dependence, or who have been sentenced for violent or sexual offences. An important aspect of this development work is the construction of a general conceptual framework to enhance the quality of special personal change programmes and facilitate evaluations of their effectiveness. In addition, a working group consisting of co-ordinators drawn from the regions and the central administration are reviewing and revising the policy and guidelines for education and training in Swedish prisons. An important basis for this work has been provided by the replies to a questionnaire addressed to all prisoners on their needs and interests concerning work, education and personal change programmes. There was a 75 per cent response rate to this questionnaire. It has generated a considerable volume of useful information which is in the process of analysis. The results of the questionnaire enquiry were presented at the end of 1996.

Chapter Eleven

Then and now: approaches to correctional education in the United States

Thom Gehring, Marilyn McShane and Carolyn Eggleston, Centre for the Study of Correctional Education, California State University, San Bernadino, USA

> *A small number of persons are doing yeoman work in an alien environment. Corrections is designed for custody and control. Education's purpose is freedom, growth, and self-actualisation. The correctional educator must, at the minimum, maintain an island of sanity in a storm of psychosis. (Reagen and Stoughton, 1976: 28).*

This chapter has three parts. The first addresses some of the major attributes of corrections in the United States and establishes a context for the rest of the chapter. The next summarises the more than 200-year history of correctional education, and introduces readers to some of the problems and concerns of correctional education professionalisation. The last part reviews some of the connections between the education of confined learners and the local schools. The second and third parts present different sequences of historical information, organised by subject.

The context of the criminal justice system

Observers from many nations are familiar with the major parameters of justice in the United States. News about corrections is replete with the words 'guns,' 'gangs,' 'drugs,' 'violence,' and information about increased numbers of juvenile and female offenders. The purpose of the next few pages is to get beyond some of these quick summaries, to emerging trends in corrections.

The structure of corrections in the US differs from that of many nations. Inmates are assigned to a system according to the law that was broken, rather than by the duration of sentence. A person who breaks a state law will be detained in a local facility until trial, then sentenced to a state institution. A person who breaks a Federal law will be assigned to a Federal institution.

The Federal system – the Federal Bureau of Prisons – is only one part of a vast network of interlocking yet separate systems. In 1993, 78,000 inmates were assigned to Federal Bureau institutions (Simonsen, in McShane and Williams,

1996: 205). Most of the Bureau's facilities are called Federal Correctional Institutions.

The greatest proportion of inmates in the US are housed in state facilities. Most states have separate agencies to incarcerate juveniles and adults. A few have a combined agency that incarcerates both juveniles and adults in separate institutions. Most adult institutions are known as state prisons; juvenile institutions are known by various names. 'Jail' usually denotes a county or local facility for adults.

In addition, there are many private facilities that house inmates for a *per diem* fee, and the nation is scattered with group homes – residential facilities for juveniles – that range from private to state-funded. Some states have vast systems of 'court schools', which are local prisons for juveniles. In California's Los Angeles County there are more juveniles assigned to residential facilities than there are adult inmates in most state systems.

The dilemma of correctional crowding has created a wealth of descriptive cliches ranging from a 'runaway train' to a prison 'building frenzy.' There are over 1.5 million people incarcerated in the US, with an additional 3.5 million under some type of community supervision (Bureau of Justice Statistics, April, 1995). During the last two decades the average annual increase of prison and jail populations has been at least 8.5 per cent. The incarceration rate in the United States is currently more than 500 per 100,000 with seven out of every 100 adult black males finding themselves in prison or jail (Criminal Justice Newsletter, September 15, 1993: 6). Likewise juvenile corrections staff report those incarcerated are ten times more likely to be minority youths than whites (Criminal Justice Newsletter, December 1, 1995: 7). Drug offenders make up 46 per cent of new prison admissions (Elvin, 1995: 5–6).

The purpose of corrections

The American correctional system, in both philosophy and operations, is fraught with controversy and irony. After years of being described as in 'crisis' by both outside critics and its own key decision makers, the system has settled into a routine of policies and practices designed to insure its continued, albeit dysfunctional, existence. The only agreement between experts is that the system itself is growing exponentially and consuming a disproportionate amount of local, state, and Federal resources.

The nature of this survival mode has been the subject of much debate. How can a variety of correctional goals be balanced? Some scholars see correctional trends reflecting a 'get tough' attitude, with increasing punishments and a bias against providing offender services and programs (Zimring and Hawkins, 1995). Others see strong evidence of support for rehabilitation and increased government spending on treatment programmes (Hamm, 1996: 525–530), as well as for community restorative justice efforts (Umbreit and Smith, 1991: 192).

Media coverage of sensational criminal cases confuses perceptions about what the public really wants to do regarding offenders. Figure 11.1 shows that the results may be a series of changes to contain both regressive and progressive penal policies.

Community supervision sentences are often stereotyped as 'getting off easy' while incarceration is equated with 'justice.' This is troubling to scholars who fear the public is desensitised to the punitiveness of a wide range of punishments. In one study, legislators and policy makers attributed more punitiveness to the public and less support for rehabilitation and treatment than researchers found when actually sampling their consistencies (Gottfredson and Taylor, 1984). A number of recent studies indicated that the public continues to hold favourable attitudes toward alternatives to incarceration (Bennett, 1991: 94–95) as well as toward rehabilitation – particularly toward academic and vocational education programmes and substance abuse treatment (Cullen, Cullen and Wozniak, 1988).

The explanation for this apparent paradox is that both punitive and rehabilitative trends are operating simultaneously. Some argue that intermediate sanctions are evidence of this drive for both treatment and punishment. Examples of such sanctions are intensive, community-based surveillance and supervision with fines; restitution; community service; and drug treatment. Others suggest intermediate sanctions can be tougher and more punitive – as well as less costly and more effective – than traditional incarceration (Petersilia, 1995; Petersilia and Deschenes, 1994: 3–8).

From all sides of American government, judicial, legislative, and administrative authorities are sending contradictory messages about what is wrong with the correctional system and what needs to be done to improve it. Often the 'best' solutions depend on whether one's priorities are reducing recidivism: saving money: or lowering public safety risks. While these priorities may not be mutually exclusive, it is clear that the system is trying to do too much, for too many, with insufficient resources.

Evaluation and effectiveness

The question of effectiveness continues to plague correctional administrators, programme evaluators, and the taxpaying public. Fortunately, more sophisticated research methodologies and a sensitivity toward complex rehabilitation issues have allowed us to examine correctional programming in more detail than ever before.

The previous generation of 'what works?' studies, many with imperfect designs and unsophisticated methodologies, often produced findings that were seized by ideologues to minimise programming. Guided by more specific questions, recent studies scrutinised a variety of treatment approaches and formats. In one meta-analysis (Andrews *et al*, 1991), researchers concluded that effective treatment programmes, regardless of specific focus, should have

Table 11.1 Mixed signals about justice issues

	Increases in Access to Programmes and Services; treatment Oriented trends	Decreases in Access to Programmes and Services; 'get tough' Policies
Courts	• Remedies for the mentally ill are expanded • Protection against unconstitutional conditions are expanded • Remedies for women faced with non-equitable programmes/services	• Upheld sex registration laws • Upheld inmate co-payment procedure for some medical or treatment services • Upheld random drug tests of inmates • Upheld mandatory policy to participate in Narcotics or Alcoholics Anonymous, to get in family reunification programme (NY)
Legislature	• Increased spending on drug treatment programmes • Mandatory treatment laws • Indeterminate sentences for mentally ill sex offenders • Religious Freedom Restoration Act • Funding for programmes to reduce gang activity	• Limits on appeals/grievances • Limits on lawsuits/writs • More groups excluded from probation and parole • Elimination of higher education grants • Repeal of inmate rights • Legislation to facilitate juvenile transfer to adult court and prison systems
Correctional Policy Administrators	• Increase in number of drug treatment programmes • Increase in cognitive treatment programme • Wider range visitation programmes • Emphasis on literacy programmes • Increase in AIDS programming • More parent/child ties and reunification programmes • More access/services on death row	• Limits on conjugal visits • Restrictions on recreation • Assessing fees for services and supervision

psychological evaluations and deliver appropriate correctional services. Another research team reported that a variety of effective approaches – particularly those that followed a cognitive-behavioural conceptual model and had multifaceted programming – worked with variables related to re-offending (Antonowicz and Ross, 1994: 97–104). After years of examining rehabilitative programmes in depth, (Palmer, 1991 and 1992) one researcher concluded new programmes should be sensitive to client needs/characteristics, and the best modalities are growth-centred interventions.

Attempts to develop the most effective intervention strategies are complicated by changing perceptions of who the high-risk/high-need populations are. Who should get the limited available resources? High-risk populations and security/safety advocates compete with rehabilitation for scarce allotments of supervision and services. Over the years the high-risk population has expanded to include those involved with gangs, guns, and violent crime, and all types of sex offenders. Will the general public be scared into targeting one or more of these groups, thereby shifting the resource distribution? High-needs offenders often have to wait for a high profile case to elicit moral indignation and shift resources back to treatment needs. High-needs groups include females, the mentally ill, the disabled, and drug and alcohol abusers.

These themes establish a background for corrections in the United States. Institutional educators are painfully familiar with the political, philosophical, and policy inhibitors to effective programming. The 'punishment only' mode makes education difficult, a situation exacerbated by resource inadequacy. The job of correctional educators is to help individuals leave the institutions better than they were when they arrived, despite debilitating social conditions and system-wide failures. The rest of this chapter is about how the field of correctional education developed in the US, and some of its current trends.

Historical themes of correctional education

Correctional Education Association (CEA) founder Austin MacCormick and other early CEA leaders maintained that the term 'correctional education' derived not from the institutions in which programmes operate, but from the inherent goals of the field. Correctional educators apply the principle that attitudes, ideas, and behaviour can be changed – that humans are capable of transforming their lives. Historically, prison reformers and correctional educators shared a common goal: to reform prisons and prisoners. This relationship is not limited to a theoretical perspective. It is expressed in the historic links and shared traditions of prison reform and correctional education.

Some European origins of the early reform years

Prisons for confined adult and juvenile populations are a relatively modern phenomenon. The first important decades of the field are known as the reform period – the last decades of the 18th and the first decades of the 19th Century.

There could be no prison reform or correctional education until there were prisons, and the establishment of prisons was actually a reform. Incarceration provided an alternative to punishments such as death, mutilation, torture, banishment, or heavy fines borne by the criminal's family. Early efforts to establish institutions and programmes were influenced by important personalities: we will focus on the contributions of John Howard, John Henry Pestalozzi, and Elizabeth Fry.

John Howard was elected sheriff of Bedford, England, just before the American Revolution. He visited exemplary institutions in Great Britain and the Continent and wrote a state-of-the-art report on how to manage gaols. Howard recommended that prisoners should be classified and separated to prevent hardened criminals from contaminating other offenders. He also recommended that jailers should be salaried. Previously, unsalaried jailers lived off fees paid by prisoners' families, and by selling food, clothes, even medical treatment, alcohol, and sexual access.

Howard's report was taken seriously by reformers who wanted to implement prisons. It came at a time when Americans were rejecting the European tradition of torture, and was especially embraced by Quakers in Pennsylvania and New York. They established new institutions and tried to live up to the standards Howard suggested.

The Pennsylvania system of prison management had convicts absolutely separated in solitary confinement. Inmates worked alone in their cells, and chaplains came to them individually for religious and instructional activities. The problem was that solitary confinement debilitates, and inmates were frequently insane by the time they were released. The New York system of prison management was also known as the Auburn system, after the first institution that was constructed exclusively for its implementation. Auburn inmates worked by day in enforced silence in prison factories and returned to individual cells at night. The problem was that Auburn institutions were very rigid and the spirit of surveillance permeated life in confinement.

These two systems greatly influenced the development of correctional education, since other states followed the examples of Pennsylvania and New York. Cell study was the rule in Pennsylvania facilities, but group learning activities were sometimes allowed in Auburn institutions.

Advocates maintained their system was the only way to implement John Howard's recommendations. A heated debate arose in the new American nation about which system was best. Correctional education was an important part of the debate, since Auburn advocates officially insisted that their system was best because more instruction could be pursued where prisoners were allowed to congregate. However, the hidden agenda that really influenced the debate was economic rather than educational. Auburn system factories were more profitable than Pennsylvania system individualised cottage industries. Legislators soon learned that Auburn-style factory institutions put money into the state treasuries, allowing them to limit taxation and ensure re-election.

Meanwhile in Switzerland, John Henry Pestalozzi implemented Rousseau's educational philosophy, and established juvenile institutions to teach war orphans after the French Revolution and Napoleonic Wars. He based his curriculum on love and worked to establish a homelike atmosphere in which children could learn from their experiences in a supportive setting. Pestalozzi gained great influence in teacher preparation. Froebel, the man who invented the kindergarten, was a disciple of Pestalozzi.

Elizabeth Fry advocated individualised literacy instruction, work, and other programmes for women throughout Great Britain and Europe during the early decades of the 19th century. Her literacy work began in 1809. She was a Quaker with influential contacts on both sides of the Atlantic and advocated implementation of John Howard's recommendations – classify and separate inmates; salary jailers. Almost single-handedly, Elizabeth Fry helped government leaders throughout Europe see the merit of establishing prisons instead of torturing criminals. She also emphasised teaching basic literacy skills so convicts could read the Bible and be 'saved for Christ.' Much of her advocacy work emphasised the Pennsylvania system, a cause to which the Quaker communities in America and England rallied during first half of the 19th century.

These early reformers promoted prison reform and correctional education as a single programme to improve the world. Nevertheless, the reform period was marked by divergent emphases. The fields of prison reform and correctional education were just beginning. Crusading Americans took the developments in Europe very seriously, and determined to improve on them in their own country.

Prison reform and education in the United States

The North American correctional education movement began in 1789, when clergyman William Rogers first offered instruction at Philadelphia's Walnut Street Jail. The warden was worried that a riot might result from this revolutionary initiative. He required that two armed guards attend the meeting with a loaded cannon aimed at the convict students. Everything was peaceful, but the incident symbolised the on-going struggle of teaching within prison walls. Despite this unseemly beginning, adult and juvenile correctional education has been on the 'cutting edge' of publicly funded education for more than 200 years.

Brief chronology of American correctional education history

There have been eight major periods of correctional education history in the US, each with its own identifiable themes.

Table 11.2: Periods of correctional education history in the U.S.

1789– 1875	Sabbath school period; Pennsylvania (solitary confinement) and Auburn (factory model) system of prison management; correctional education is possible
1876– 1900	Zebulon Brockway's tenure at Elmira Reformatory, bringing together the themes emphasised by Maconochie (near Australia), Crofton (Ireland), and the Pilsburys (United States); the beginnings of correctional/special education; reformatory movement efforts to transform prisons into schools
1901– 1929	The development of prison libraries, and reformatories for women; democratic patterns of correctional education – William George, Thomas Mott Osborne, and Austin MacCormick; Anton Makarenko's work begins in the Soviet Union
1930– 1941	'The golden age of correctional education'; MacCormick's programmes and professionalisation influence; the New York and Federal experiments; rebirth of correctional/special education; Kenyon Scudder begins his tenure as reform warden of an important experimental prison without walls
1946– 1964	Recovery from the interruption of World War II; the themes of Glenn Kendall's work extend those of MacCormick, and set the pace for Cold War correctional education
1965– 1980	Key improvements and centres of correctional education; the Federal influence in education; post-secondary programmes, state-wide correctional school districts; special education legislation; correctional teacher preparation programmes
1981– 1988	Conservative trend in Federal influence and many states; rise of Correctional Education Association influence; continuation of trends from the previous period; Ross and Fabiano's definitive book on progress in Canada and the US
1989	The current period, with its emphasis on culture(s) and humanities, developmental education; rise of international co-operation; information access to inform correctional educators of their history/literature and promote professional networking; nevertheless, many systems continue traditional programmes; growth of mandatory attendance for adults.

Many of these themes cannot be developed in this chapter. Instead, the following sections introduce some of the main contributions, to give an overview of salient trends.

Most American prison reformers during the years from 1789 to 1875 shared strong religious convictions. They wanted to teach convicts literacy skills so they could read the Bible and be 'saved'. Part-time volunteer chaplains organised early correctional education programmes according to the 'Sabbath school' model. Prototypic Sunday schools were implemented in many north-eastern states.

These improvements paralleled reform efforts on the other side of the Atlantic by Pestalozzi and Fry. They were facilitated by professional networking associations catering to the needs of prison reformers and correctional educators. First amongst these associations was the Philadelphia Society for the Alleviation of the Miseries of Public Prisons, which advocated for the Pennsylvania system. Next came the Boston Prison Discipline Society, which advocated the Auburn system. Finally, the Prison Association of New York eventually advocated for reformatory prison discipline – a system that will be introduced in the next section.

Reformatory prison discipline

Though geographically separated, advocates of this period knew their work was linked; each admired Captain Alexander Maconochie at Norfolk Island, a penal colony in the British South Pacific between Australia and New Zealand. During the years 1840–1844 Maconochie established indeterminate sentences, progressive housing, vocational education, and parole. He called his system Reformatory Prison Discipline, as an alternative to harsh brutality.

In Ireland, Sir Walter Crofton declared himself a disciple of Maconochie, and implemented Reformatory Prison Discipline nationwide. Mary Carpenter, an Englishwoman who organised correctional educators from juvenile institutions and adult prisons, wrote on Crofton's innovations. The Irish developments, and Carpenter's books on them, won devotion from prison leaders in the US.

Foremost amongst these American advocates was Zebulon Brockway. He was affiliated with the Pilsburys, who established a family-oriented 'dynasty' that controlled most prisons in the United States. The Pilsburys championed the Auburn system, but they identified its deficiencies at about the same time that news about Maconochie's system became available through Crofton and Carpenter.

Throughout his long career, Brockway had prison reform advocates and tough-minded prison managers working together to implement better correctional education. Today, a feat like that seems impossible. The Reformatory Movement, from 1870 to about 1900, was the result. It was a massive effort to change prisons into schools by emphasising education. At its height, the Elmira

Reformatory (NY) school offered training in 42 vocational trades and elementary, secondary, even post-secondary academic training.

During the 1880s and 1890s, Elmira Reformatory superintendent Brockway implemented educational programmes for disabled learners. The categories of disabilities were different from the ones we apply today: dullards; weaklings; awkwards; the exceptionally stupid in one academic function; incorrigibles; kindergartners; stupids; and so forth. However, the methods were somewhat parallel to current practice, and in some cases perhaps more advanced. The special education staff included physicians; craftsmen; professors; attorneys; and teachers (Brockway, 1912/1969).

Citizenship and democracy

The subsequent period emphasised democracy. In North America democracy is believed to be mutually exclusive from prisons, because institutions are populated with offenders and managed to emphasise custody and control. However, there is a history of success in democratic prisons. In this tradition, the work of William George, Thomas Mott Osborne, and Austin MacCormick are most significant.

George started a Long Island summer camp for New York City youth in 1895. It soon became a year-round juvenile institution for boys and girls, known as the Junior Republic. George encouraged the children to manage every aspect of the institution except the school, which was regulated by State law. This included financial and personnel decisions, and programme development. The Junior Republic was administered according to the principles of the US Constitution. Wards elected representatives, senators, and a president who appointed a supreme court to handle disciplinary matters. Thomas Mott Osborne served on the Republic board and was appointed to its Supreme Court. The Republic was co-educational; its legislature enfranchised girls before the 19th Amendment which extended the right to vote to American women (George, 1911).

A millionaire industrialist and politician, Osborne disguised himself as a prisoner in 1913 to learn first-hand about conditions at Auburn, the famous prison in his home town. Osborne helped organise the Mutual Welfare League, a democratic, inmate-controlled organisation. With the warden's permission, the League managed every dimension of the prison. Disciplinary problems were nearly eliminated, and production in the prison shops increased markedly. By providing daily experiences in democracy and responsible social interaction, Osborne successfully transformed a loathsome maximum security prison into an uplifting education–oriented institution. Then he was assigned as warden at Sing Sing. The inmates there established a great school, the Mutual Welfare Academy. During World War I, Osborne was appointed warden of the US Naval Prison at Portsmouth, New Hampshire. Many inmates were rehabilitated and served their country before the War ended (Tannenbaum, 1933).

Osborne trained Austin MacCormick, who based his correctional education theories on those of Brockway and Osborne. MacCormick's book led to the correctional education 'renaissance' of the 1930s. He was the first assistant director of the Federal Bureau of Prisons, travelling around the country to establish or expand prison schools and libraries. For 50 years MacCormick provided leadership at The Osborne Association Inc, one of the nation's most active prison reform organisations. He founded the Correctional Education Association and was the first editor of the *Journal of Correctional Education*. World War II interrupted professional development in correctional education, and then the Cold War constrained it.

Cold War crisis

In the Soviet Union, after the Revolution and the subsequent Civil War, Anton Makarenko founded 'Gorky Colonies' to house and educate war orphans and young criminals. Maxim Gorky was Makarenko's mentor and editor; out of gratitude the term Gorky Colony was established. Makarenko emphasised the civic responsibilities of 'the New Soviet Man,' through social education and many social education activities (Makarenko, 1973). He is known as the 'John Dewey of the Soviet Union,' which means that his ideas shaped Soviet local education. Dewey and Makarenko corresponded for years – Dewey made several pilgrimages to Makarenko, and they made a film together about the proper way to educate at-risk students.

In New York, Glenn Kendall established the State's first adult reception and diagnostic centre at the old Elmira facility. Kendall wrote the definitive book on social education and promoted special education from the mid 1930s to the mid 1960s. In California, reform warden Kenyon Scudder established a 'prison without walls' in 1941, and helped put educators in charge of educational decisions. Scudder staffed the California Institution for Men according to merit – a departure from the prevailing political system. This was the first implementation of MacCormick's 'Red Barn' theory: we can establish an effective prison in an old red barn, if it is staffed correctly. Skudder was warden until 1956. The 1960s and 1970s were influenced substantially by John McKee and Tony Ryan. McKee's work began at Draper Correctional Institution in Elmore, Alabama. He focuses on individualising instruction and technological applications. Tony Ryan's nationwide work began out of Hawaii and then shifted to South Carolina. She focuses on adult and career education in corrections.

The post-Cold War culture period

During the post-Cold War period the emphasis shifted to teams of contributors rather than single heroes. This period is known as the culture period, with an important emphasis on the ability of culture(s) to help people stay out of prison. Culture(s) informs us how to live decently in community; subcultures tend to focus on drugs, gangs, guns, and violence. Many people work to improve correctional education, but our focus will be on those who have also contributed most to the growing, relevant literature.

The first post-Cold War team worked separately, on similar themes. Emphasis on humanities instruction increased, along with participatory management; cognitive, cognitive-moral, and cognitive-democratic psychologies; and other related themes. Robert Ross (Canada) responded to Martinson's 1974 declaration that 'nothing works' to rehabilitate confined criminals. Ross and Elizabeth Fabiano launched a comprehensive study to identify 'what works, and why?' and then wrote the definitive book on the subject, *Time to Think* (1985), which anticipated the post-Cold War period.

Post-secondary programmes at Federal institutions around Vancouver were seen as an exemplary by Ross and Fabiano. These programmes were managed by Stephen Duguid, whose developmental humanities and social science courses for inmates were a great encouragement to many correctional educators. Duguid also edited the *Yearbook of Correctional Education* and founded the International Forum for the Study of Education in Penal Systems (IFEPS). These Canadian innovations were taken seriously in the United States, and many systems looked to them as programme models.

In California, David Werner applied parallel systems and managed the CEAs Postsecondary Special Interest Group. His *Correctional Education Theory and Practice* (1990) clearly articulated culture period emphases and has helped many in the field.

The California team of Carolyn Eggleston and Thom Gehring worked with others to organise the Centre for the Study of Correctional Education. Centre activities span the areas of teacher preparation and inservice, research, and professional development. The Eggleston and Gehring team work to make the rich correctional education literature accessible. Results suggest that professional networking and study can help increase clarity of thought on correctional education issues, thereby helping practitioners feel less vulnerable to institutional constraints.

Overview of the chronological perspective

The tradition of progress will continue, but it is premature to speculate about attributes that will characterise the future of the field. The related disciplines of prison reform and correctional education have been mutually supportive, generation after generation, as expressed below in Table 11.3.

The professional identity issue

Table 11.3 demonstrated that for more than 200 years the correctional education movement has a record of step-by-step improvement. Clergymen, sociologists, psychologists, and novelists; professionals and community volunteers; 'bleeding hearts' and 'law and order' advocates have all connected the intense correctional education context with an understanding of the human adventure.

Table 11.3 Summary of correctional education historical trends

Period	Main Contributors	Contributions	Time Period	Summary Statements
Reform	John Howard	First state-of-the-art prison reform handbook	Before/after American Revolution	Salary jailers; classify and separate prisoners
	John Henry Pestalozzi	Educated Swiss war orphans	Turn of the 19th century	Psychologise education
	Elizabeth Fry	Advocated individualised education, work	1809–1830s	Pennsylvania system; literacy (read the Bible, be 'saved')
Prison Reform	Alexander Maconochie	Progressive housing, vocational education, indeterminate sentences,	1840–1844	Reformatory Prison Discipline
	Sir Walter Crofton		Before US Civil War	Irish system of prison discipline
	Zebulon Brockway	parole; other innovations	1876–1900	'The educational idea of it all'
Citizenship/ Democracy	William George	Democratic management of institutions by elected wards or inmates including discipline with the warden's permission	1895–1909	'Citizenship is our standard'
	Thomas Mott Osborne		1913–1926	The New Penology, 'better citizens'
	Austin MacCornick		1915–1979	Grunhut's Adult education model; citizenship socialisation
Cold War	Anton Makarenko	Educated youth for Communism	1922–mid 1930s	The New Soviet Man; social education
	Glenn Kendall	Special education; group learning	1939–1973	diagnostic-prescripion method, social education
	Kenyon Scudder	Put educators in charge of education	1941–1956, at CA Institute for Men	Prisoners are people; Red Barn personnel theory
Culture	Ross Fabiano, Stephen Duguid, and David Werner	Education of whole person; personal responsibility ethical decision-making	1980s and 1990s . . .	Humanities; developmental learning for maturation partic management; 'New Paradigm'/Center for the Study of
	Eggleston & Gehring	international professionalisation	1980s and 1990s . . .	Corrective education

But in the US the record indicates correctional educators themselves may be the last to appreciate their own work.

Institutional teachers were always slow to identify professionally with the correctional education field. Instead, they identified with the related disciplines: the chaplaincy; higher education; common schools; and vocational education. Adult education; social work; and correspondence courses each had their heyday. For decades particular aspects of the public school model predominated, almost like fads: educational counselling; career and special education; distance learning and computer applications. Recently boot camps, an industrial emphasis, mandatory literacy and other control-oriented fads took centre stage. Correctional educators have always accepted the identity of any professional discipline except the one that fits best – correctional education. This phenomenon is called the 'confused identity problem.'

The CEA has launched a vigorous program to provide information and profession-wide leadership to overcome the confused identity problem, and to consolidate the field. The CEA has a staffed, national headquarters near Washington DC. Legislative action to improve correctional education has resulted in some important successes, even during budgetary cutbacks. The CEA has undergone intensive, participatory self-study, with resolutions and long-range plans. The Association is a network of professionals, complete with its own journal, national newsletter, a *Yearbook*, a host of regional and statewide periodicals, regular conferences, and well-organised special interest groups.[1]

Connections with the local schools

In the US rights are written into law. Since the US Constitution contains no mention of it, education fits under the 'reserved powers' clause of the Tenth Amendment. This clause reserves to the states all powers not specifically delegated to the states or prohibited to them in the Constitution. (Ornstein and Levine, 1993: 159). Education began in the Colonies, of course, but Federal support for education received renewed emphasis during the mid-1960s, as part of President Lyndon Johnson's War on Poverty. In 1991 approximately 49 per cent of all funds for local education were from State sources, 45 per cent were from local sources, and 6 per cent was from Federal sources (Ornstein and Levine, 1993: 235).

The Federal Bureau of Prisons cannot use the traditional Federal funding sources to support its education programmes. However, state correctional educa-tion systems can use these funds. Since the mid-1960s, in addition to state monies, state prison and juvenile institution schools have used Federal funding sources, especially from the following programmes: Elementary and Secondary

[1]The association is affiliated with the American Correctional Association. For more information, contact: Dr Stephen Steurer, CEA Executive Director; 4380 Forbes Boulevard; Lanham, Maryland 20706. Or telephone: (301) 918–1915

Education Act, for neglected and delinquent children under the age of 21; Vocational Education Act; Special Education funds, mostly for youth, explained below; Adult Education Act, adults only, mostly applicable 'inside' for adult basic education (literacy and numeracy).

In addition, some funding sources have come and gone. The Rehabilitative Services Act was applicable to help inmates learn, but has been discontinued. The Basic Educational Opportunities Act, later renamed the Pell Act, helped fund post-secondary education for the poor, including inmates. However, in the mid 1990s Pell grants for inmates were discontinued. The Library Services Construction Act was used to fund institutional libraries, but recent regulatory changes have made this difficult.

Special education has a long history in the US and marks a point of departure from education in many nations. In its current configuration, as set forth in Public Law 94–142 (1975 – The Education of All Handicapped Children Act, or EHA), special education applies only to students who are educationally disadvantaged.

> *The EHA was designed to correct the lack of programs for educationally disabled children and youth aged five through twenty-one in the public schools. It states that disabled students, wherever they are found, must be provided a 'free, appropriate, public education' . . . A disabled student's placement in a correctional facility is specifically included under the EHA . . . Eleven categories were established under which students could be found eligible for special education. A student must fit into one or more of the categories to qualify for special education. The eleven categories are specific learning disability, serious emotional disturbance, mental retardation, hearing impaired/deaf, visually impaired/blind, multiply handicapped, communication handicapped, other health impaired, orthopedically handicapped, physically handicapped, and speech impaired. (Eggleston and Gehring, in McShane and Williams, 1996, p. 188).*

The EHA was reauthorised and strengthened in 1990 as the Individuals with Disabilities Education Act (IDEA). Special education services are assigned by a multidisciplinary team. The services are organised to emphasise confidentiality of information and the least restrictive environment for education. Many states have been found 'out of compliance', with regard to Federal and also state special education laws. How to provide these services effectively remains a controversial issue.

Another controversial issue is whether correctional schools are real schools, subject to the rights and obligations of local schools. In the US local schools are organised as Local Education Agencies (LEAs), overseen by State Educational Agencies (SEAs), consistent with the US Constitution's reserved powers clause.

Until the late 1920s the decentralised organisation of correctional schools attracted little attention. New York State governor Franklin Delano Roosevelt established a cadre of educational supervisors in the State corrections office.

Under Austin MacCormick's leadership, the Federal Bureau of Prisons implemented a similar structure. A result of these models was that education became more visible within state correctional organisations and educators had somewhat more authority over educational decisions. Today, this model is called a bureau. It is better than the antecedent, decentralised 'system', in which non-educators were always in control of educational decisions. By the 1970s half the states had implemented correctional education bureaus.

In the late 1960s, beginning in Texas and Connecticut, state systems of prisons and juvenile institutions began to organise correctional school districts (CSDs). Today 22 statewide organisations have CSDs. Their main feature is that the SEA treats the correctional education service delivery organisation as an LEA, with all the rights and obligations of any other LEA or local public school system. This innovation extends eligibility to funds that support education, and official recognition for learning that takes place in 'inside' schools. It requires a host of personnel qualifications and programme quality standards. In short, a CSD has 'real schools', according to all the parameters of schools in the local community, instead of merely having educational programmes to suggest to the public that rehabilitation is being pursued.

For the most part, schools in local facilities – jails, group homes, and court schools – are offered directly by the LEA in the jurisdiction in which the institution is located. The issue of who provides educational services in these institutions – educators or 'jailers' – is not usually as relevant in local institutions as it is in state and Federal facilities.

Despite recent improvements, most correctional education programmes in the US focus on basic academic skills – literacy and numeracy – and vocational skills. Schooling in the United States follows the example of John Dewey, who held that socialisation and education should take place simultaneously, in the same space. In many nations socialisation – how to survive and live in a community – is separated from education, the culture that is passed from one generation to the next. In American prisons and institutions for juveniles, the focus has been on socialisation – how to read; how to write; basic arithmetic; and job skill development. Until very recently, emphasis on culture(s) has been systematically minimised.

One popular way to express the different needs between education in local and correctional schools has been to examine the traditional 'formula' for American education. In the local schools, that formula is 'knowledge, skills, and attitudes', in that priority order. The formula for correctional education should be precisely the reverse: 'attitudes, skills, and knowledge'. In this difference, the move from traditional emphasis on socialisation to an emphasis on culture may be long overdue. The following paragraphs outline attributes of instruction and learning in US corrections and how they relate to American schooling in general.

Many modern educational practices began in correctional education

The Common School movement of the mid 1800s led to the American public school system. Efforts to refine and improve public education began almost immediately, in response to the changing nature of the United States. A group of prominent urban school reformers addressed local school delivery patterns before and during World War I. Amongst these was educator David Snedden. His influence was based on the data and principles he collected from reformatory schools. Snedden studied juvenile correctional education for his dissertation at Columbia University and identified models for replication in other educational settings. Originally, Snedden and other urban school reformers were interested in reformatory schools because they provided 'laboratories' for compulsory attendance. The reformers aspired to implement compulsory education for children nationwide, to solve the problem of roving bands of street children who created havoc.

Soon, however, reformers found additional reasons to study correctional education. Snedden assumed that successful programmes in the most restrictive educational environment would flourish elsewhere. In his 1907 book *Administration and Educational Work of American Juvenile Reform Schools* he reported on pioneer models of vocational – especially trade and industrial – physical; and, military education – boot camps – and summarised how public school educators could learn from correctional teachers. Many of these models became the antecedents of local school practice.

At the 1938 American Association of School Administrators conference in Atlantic City, approximately 2,000 people attended a session on 'Reduction in Crime Through Improved Public Educational Programs and the Educational Rehabilitation of Prison Inmates' – but there was room for only 700. Improvised loud speakers were installed in corridors, lobbies, and adjoining rooms, so interested participants could hear. Articles about this unprecedented level of interest appeared in *Harper's* Magazine and *School Executive*. At the next year's conference in Cleveland the correctional education session brought in over 8,000 people.

Currently, local school educators know that their colleagues in institutions address the same problems they themselves find so frustrating. In a coercive setting those problems are even more difficult than in local schools. Correctional educators work with students who have dropped out, been pushed out or experienced repeated failure in the local schools. They are often embittered and apathetic or alienated, with histories of violence or sexual problems, and with poor self-concept. They can also be students who lack study skills and have a high incidence of learning, or emotional problems (43 per cent); and drug-related problems (75 per cent); in confined populations. The environments in training schools, reformatories, and prisons are often bleak and antithetical to the educational mission. Outside observers expect these conditions to minimise student learning. Yet most correctional education programmes are successful according to traditional measures of learning. In 1980, these facts prompted the US Education Department to establish a Correctional Education office, by announcing the following ideas:

> . . . *programs which can succeed in this most difficult setting can be replicable in less restrictive environments. Toward this end, correctional education should be viewed as a laboratory for testing relevant models which can be disseminated to other contexts. (Gehring, 1980).*

The systematic development of individualised instruction

Historically, Aristotle taught students individually and 'little red schoolhouse' teachers used individualised activities. However, the individually prescribed instruction (IPI) method was systematically applied and later perfected at prison and reformatory schools. John Howard advocated individualised classification in England in the 1780s. Prison reformers championed individualisation because it enhances meaningful treatment and the reformation of criminals.

The IPI method has been closely linked in theory to the medical model of corrections: an authority figure clinically diagnoses offender deficits, prescribes remedial programming, and monitors inmate progress toward being 'cured'. The IPI method we know today started as a correctional education innovation, and was later adopted by local public schools. Consider these events: The New York law that established Elmira Reformatory, drafted by Brockway, required school records be maintained on each student; Austin MacCormick wrote on the systematic individualisation of instruction in his book *The Education of Adult Prisoners* (1931). The history of IPI was reviewed by New York City associate superintendent of schools William Grady, in 1939: ' . . . the pioneers in . . . classification and individualisation of personality were the prisons rather than the schools. My hat's off to the prisons.' (APA, 1939: 61). During the 1960s and 1970s, when IPI was accepted widely in the local schools, Dr John McKee's experiments at Draper Correctional Institution documented its success in correctional education.

The IPI method was designed to address severe basic skill deficits in heterogeneous correctional populations. It was one by-product of correctional education. Similarly, the roots of modern physical and vocational education practices have been traced to correctional education.

The emerging trend

The emerging North American paradigm in correctional education focuses on culture(s) – it both subsumes and transcends the current emphases on basic and marketable skills. Culture period correctional education takes a 'whole student' perspective, using a developmental approach, to help students grow and mature toward personal responsibility and ethical decision-making. In this effort the work of Ross and Fabiano, Duguid, and Werner stand out; Eggleston and

Gehring helped extend and consolidate the trend. Additional contributions will be made by correctional education practitioner/writers within the prison reform/correctional education school of thought. But it is too early to anticipate their specific contributions. We live in a period of deep cultural transformation. Though we may develop clarity about the trend's general direction, we do not know what will happen next.

Conclusion

Correctional education in the US has been influenced by nationwide trends in corrections and education, and models from other countries. The prison reform/correctional education field has its own history and literature, heroes, and proud traditions. There has been a direction to correctional education development: from distant reform efforts; through prison reform; democratic influences; the Renaissance of the 1930s; Cold War crisis; to the current culture period. These processes are still unfolding and the field remains formative, even after more than 200 years.

References

Andrews, D A, Zinger, R D, Hoge, J B, Gendreau, P, and Cullen, T C (1991). Does correctional treatment work? A clinically relevant and psychologically-informed meta-analysis. *Criminology*, 28:369–404.

Antonowicz, D, and Ross, R (1994). Essential components of successful rehabilitation programs for offenders. *International Journal of Offender Therapy and Comparative Criminology*, 38(2) 97–104.

(APA) American Prison Association. (1930). *Proceedings of the sixtieth annual congress of the American Prison Association*. Louisville, Kentucky: APA.

Bennett, L (1991). The public wants accountability. *Corrections Today*. 53(4) 92, 94–95.

Brockway, Z (1969 – reprint of the 1912 edition). *Fifty Years of Prison Service: An Autobiography*. Montclair, New Jersey: Patterson Smith.

Bureau of Justice Statistics (April, 1995). Correctional populations in the United States. Washington, DC: US Department of Justice.

Criminal Justice Newsletter (December 1, 1995). Blacks surpass whites in prison and jail population. 26(23) 7.

Criminal Justice Newsletter (September 15, 1993). Minority custody rate 10 times that of whites in some states. 24(18) 6.

Cullen, F, Cullen, J, and Wozniak, J (1988). Is rehabilitation dead? A myth of the punitive public. *Journal of Criminal Justice*, 16 303–317.

Elvin, J (1995). 'Three strikes' laws won't reduce crime. *The National Prison Project Journal*, 10(2) 5–6.

Gehring, T (September, 1980). Correctional education and the United States Department of Education. *Journal of Correctional Education*.

George, W (1911). *The Junior Republic: Its History and Ideals*. New York: D. Appleton.

Gottfredson, S, and Taylor, R (1984). Public policy and prison population: Measuring opinions about reform. *Judicure*, 68(4–5) 190–201.

Hamm, M (1996). Incapacitation: Penal confinement and the restraint of crime, by Franklin E Zimring and Gordon Hawkins. Book review in *Justice Quarterly*, 13(3) 525–530.

MacCormick, A (1931). *The Education of Adult Prisoners*. New York: The National Society of Penal Information.

Makarenko, A S (1973). *The Road to Life: An Epic in Education*. New York: Oriole.

McShane, M, and Williams, F (1996). *Encyclopedia of American Prisons*. New York: Garland.

Ornstein, A C, and Levine, D U (1993). *Foundations of Education*. Boston, Massachusetts: Houghton Mifflin.

Palmer, T (1991). The effectiveness of intervention: Recent trends and current issues. *Crime and Delinquency*, 37, 330–346.

Palmer, T (1992). Growth-centered intervention: An overview of changes in recent decades. *Federal Probation*, 56(1) 62–67.

Petersilia, J (1995). A crime control rationale for reinvesting in community corrections. *The Prison Journal*, 75(4) 479–496.

Petersilia, J and Deschanes, E. (1994). What punishes: Inmates rank the severity of prison vs intermediate sanctions. *Federal Probation*, 58, 3–8.

Reagen, M V and Stoughton, D M (eds) (1976). *School Behind Bars: A Descriptive Overview of Correctional Education in the American Prison System*. Metuchen, New Jersey: The Scarecrow Press.

Ross, R, and Fabiano, E (1985). *Time to Think: A Cognitive Model of Delinquency Prevention and Offender Rehabilitation*. Johnson City, Tennessee: Institute of Social Sciences and Arts.

Snedden, D S (1907). *Administration and Educational Work of American Juvenile Reform Schools*. New York: Teachers College, Columbia University.

Tannenbaum, F (1933). *Osborne of Sing Sing*. Chapel: University of North Carolina Press.

Umbreit, M and Smith, L (1991). Minnesota mediation center produces positive results. *Corrections Today*, 53(5) 192.

Werner, D (1990). *Correctional Education: Theory and Practice*. Danville, Illinois: Interstate.

Zimring, F E and Hawkins, G (1995). *Incapacitation: Penal Confinement and the Restraint of Crime*. New York: Oxford University Press.

Glossary

AEVTI	Adult Education and Vocational Training Institute
ANTA	Australian National Training Authority
APEL	Accreditation of Prior Experiential Learning
APL	Accreditation of Prior Learning
AVTS	Australian Vocational Training System
BEAT	Bridging Education and Training
CEA	Correctional Education Association
CGEA	Certificate of General Education for Adults
CSC	Correctional Service of Canada
CSD	Correctional School of Canada
CZZK	Central Board of Penitentiaries (Poland)
DEET	Commonwealth Department of Employment Education and Training
EHA	Education of All Handicapped Children Act
EPEA	European Prison Education Association
FE	Further Education
GDR	German Democratic Republic
GENEPT	The Student's Association of Voluntary Aid for Prisoners (France)
IDEA	Individuals with Disabilities Education Act
IFEPS	International Forum for the Study of Education in Penal Systems
IPI	Individually Prescribed Instruction
LAEA	Latvian Adult Education Association
LEA	Local Education Agency (United States)
LEA	Local Education Authority (Great Britian)
NBEET	National Board on Employment Education and Training
NVQ	National Vocational Qualification
QCSC	Queensland Corrective Services Commission
RCMP	Royal Canadian Mounted Police
RSC	Royal Shakespeare Company
SEA	State Educational Agency
SIR	Statistical Information on Recidivism
TAFE	Colleges of Technical and Further Education
USSR	Union of Soviet Socialist Republic
VET	Vocational Education and Training
VETAB	Vocational Education and Training Advisory Body
VETEC	Queensland Vocational Education, Training and Employment Commission
WORC	Western Outreach Camps

Also published by NIACE

Adults Learning
ISSN 0955 2308
Published ten times a year

UK subscription rates: £40 institutions; £25 individuals; £15 part-time tutors and students. Multiple subscriptions: £15 per extra copy. Overseas: add 25% airmail, 10% surface mail.

The need for a journal for adult learning professionals has never been greater. Most students in further and higher education in Britain are adults. More awareness of the importance of adults is being shown by government, media, employers and trade unions. In a quickly-changing environment it is vital to keep abreast of current issues and initiatives, debates and events.

Adults Learning is the only UK-wide journal devoted to matters concerning adult learning. It carries the latest news on policy and practice. It is a forum for adult educators to exchange information, share practice, network and engage in dialogue with fellow professionals.

Forthcoming books from NIACE

Excluded men
Veronica McGivney
ISBN 1 86201 039 0
1998 forthcoming, approx 80pp, £12.00

Although surveys usually show that more men than women are involved in post-compulsory education and training, this is largely accounted for by employer- and government-supported training. Men with low literacy levels and few qualifications are under-represented in all forms of education and training. Social and economic trends suggest that the issue of male participation is a matter of urgency. This book looks at barriers to participation and implications for targeting and curriculum approaches, with examples of effective practice.

Transforming knowledge: feminism and adult education
Jean Barr
ISBN 1 86201 046 3
1999 forthcoming, approx 160 pp, £14.95

This book suggests that the current social, political and cultural context offers new possibilities for a reconstructed radical agenda for adult education. It seeks to redress what the author argues has been a systematic exclusion in adult education histories and textbooks of the influence of feminism. The author seeks to show that what adult education researchers and practitioners do is located within wider power relations and discourses.

A full publications catalogue is available on request from NIACE, 21 De Montfort Street, Leicester LE1 7GE, England. Alternatively, visit the NIACE website on http://www.niace.org.uk